STUDIES IN EUROPEAN UNION

No. 2 in the Series

ECONOMIC AND MONETARY UNION

Editor: **Rory O'Donnell**
Foreword: **Dr. Tomás F. Ó Cofaigh**

Authors: **Rory O'Donnell**
Patrick Honohan

Institute of European Affairs

British Library Cataloguing in Publication Data:

A catalogue record for this book is available from the British Library.

ISSN 0791–5888

ISBN 1–874109–01 X

Published by the

Institute of European Affairs,

8 North Great George's Street,

Dublin 1,

Ireland.

1991.

Typeset in 10/11 Times Roman by Ree-Pro Ltd., Dublin.

Designed by Victor McBrien.

Printed in the Republic of Ireland by O'Donoghue Print Ltd., Dublin.

CONTENTS

FOREWORD

The Institute of European Affairs honoured me by asking me to act as Chairperson of the Working Group which it was proposed to set up to carry out a study of the issues involved for the European Community, and more particularly Ireland, in the current proposals for Economic and Monetary Union. I gladly acquiesced in assisting in the Institute's objective of presenting these issues, and the options available in meeting them, in terms which would be understandable — allowing for their complex and, often, highly technical nature.

It could not be more fitting that this new Institute, which has been launched under such propitious circumstances and with such distinguished patronage and support, should choose the areas of Economic and Monetary Union, and Political Union, for immediate and apolitical study. The description of the study as apolitical was significant in that it allowed the participation in the respective Working Groups of, among others, the various proponents of national politics, participating on a personal basis and without attribution of views. I was fortunate, therefore, in my capacity as Chairperson in having, as part of the EMU Working Group, a Consultative Committee with wide political, business and academic backgrounds.

The Consultative Committee considered working papers prepared by prominent economists. Dr. Rory O'Donnell acted as coordinator and brought with him to the study a wide experience of the subject from his work on behalf of NESC, the Department of Finance and the European Commission.

Uniquely perhaps, the Working Group had access, for advice and criticism, to the major government departments concerned (Departments of the Taoiseach, Finance, Foreign Affairs and Industry and Commerce) and the Central Bank. The Group is indebted to the Taoiseach, the Ministers and Secretaries of the Departments concerned and the Governor of the Central Bank for making this liaison possible. The papers which follow in this volume, it must be said both from the point of view of the authorities and the Institute, are not intended to reflect exclusively the views of the authorities. To do so would be to fall short of the *raison d'etre* of the Working Group and the Institute itself. In the final analysis, the views expressed, and the approaches adopted in the papers, are the personal, informed, responsibility of the authors themselves.

Participation in the study provided me with great personal satisfaction. It renewed my former career involvement, while in the Department of Finance and the Central Bank, in the proceedings of the EC Monetary Committee, EcoFin, the Committee of Governors of the Community Central Banks and of the Board of Governors of the European Monetary Cooperation Fund.

I have said elsewhere — and I may not be alone in this — that the Irish decision in 1978 to enter the European Monetary System (EMS) and to adhere, notwithstanding the absence of sterling, to the Exchange Rate Mechanism (ERM) was as significant an event as was 1921, in that what the one did for political freedom, the other did for establishing our monetary and financial independence. There was no doubt in the minds of those involved in the 1978 decision that it implied, in a short space of time, breaking the long-standing link with sterling and formulating, explicitly and autonomously, Irish exchange rate, interest rate and, in general, monetary policies. That contingency happily had already received careful consideration in its own right and the consequences had been identified. The subsequent successful initiation of wholly Irish money and foreign exchange markets reflected the prior planning involved. To say all this is not to digress but to make the point that, having demonstrated our ability to deal successfully with EMS entry and, paradoxically, to derive the benefits from the constraints which entry imposed, a decision to move with the Community into closer monetary union does not hold uncharted terrors for us. That is not to dismiss lightly the problems of emerging completely from behind the defences of exchange controls nor of facing unpredictable capital movements.

The problem, as the Working Group's deliberations confirmed, is not so much the matter of EMU entry but the pace of entry and the environment of entry. Moreover, these two aspects of entry pertain to economic rather than to monetary union. Their sensitivity relates particularly to possible institutional deficiencies in the Community system and the task of developing and implementing acceptable economic (including fiscal) policies and programmes; having particular regard, because of Ireland's peripherality, to the needs of convergence and cohesion. Wide ranging sectoral interests require to be taken into account — industry, agriculture and the service industries — as well as the interaction of these with the fiscal policy parameters of an economic union. The Working Group is satisfied as a result of their examination that more work remains to be done with regard to the economic union aspects of EMU. Rather than wait until one comprehensive presentation can be made, they decided, with the approval of the Institute, that the balance of advantage lay with proceeding with the immediate publication of papers, by Rory O'Donnell and Patrick Honohan, covering the general background, monetary union and, because of its underlying general applicability, cohesion. They further decided to develop more deeply and comprehensively the issues arising in the context of economic union, including fiscal policy aspects, and to publish a second volume of papers emerging from this further study as soon as possible. This timetable may have the additional advantage that the papers can take into account on-going developments regarding the Common Agricultural Policy, and of the CAP study which has been initiated by the Institute.

Emerging from the studies is the importance of an overall strategic approach to all these matters, in conjunction with the pursuit of Irish policy in regard to political union. The National Economic and Social Council has already adverted to that need and one may safely assume that the Irish negotiators are well cognisant of it.

I hope, as Chairperson of the Working Group, that the results of their efforts as represented by the present volume and the second volume to come, may be of significant assistance in promoting informed debate about the issues at stake in Ireland's participation in the European Community's advance to economic and monetary integration.

Dr. Tomás F. Ó Cofaigh,
Chairperson,
EMU Working Group.
November, 1991, Dublin.

IDENTIFYING THE ISSUES

Rory O'Donnell

EXECUTIVE SUMMARY

Current moves to EMU are prompted by an awareness that the full benefits of the single market cannot be achieved without a single currency.

The Irish government has declared itself strongly favourable to EMU in principle.

Economic and Monetary Union requires a Treaty basis over and above that in the Treaty of Rome and the Single Act. In Ireland's case this implies a constitutional referendum.

EMU means not only a single currency but also a fully integrated single market and coordination of national macroeconomic policies. But a single market — not only for goods and services, but also for capital and labour — requires that national policies which influence competitive conditions be either harmonised or abolished. Since some favour reregulation at the Community level, and others deregulation, there is no universally agreed definition of the single market or of EMU. The scope and content of Community policies is contested by various interest groups.

In deciding to proceed to EMU the European Council adopted a number of principles concerning EMU. These are (i) *parallel* development of monetary and economic integration; (ii) *subsidiarity*; (iii) central bank independence *and price stability* as the primary objective of monetary policy.

With these principles agreed, the main issue in the design and construction of EMU is how to conduct *economic* policy. The proposed system of EMU is as follows:

Objectives:

(i) growth

(ii) a high level of employment

(iii) price stability

(iv) convergence of economic performance

(v) economic and social cohesion.

Instruments:

(i) multiannual economic guidelines

(ii) multilateral surveillance

(iii) EC financial assistance in the case of acute difficulties.

Budgetary rules:

(i) no monetary financing

(ii) no bailing out

(iii) no excessive deficits.

Most debate turns on whether these provisions are necessary and sufficient to achieve the objectives.

Discussion has tended to focus on the price stability objective: dispute centres on how much EC *control of national fiscal policy* is necessary. Opinions range from the view that the financial markets can be relied on to prevent governments running excessive deficits, to the idea that precise constitutional rules on budget deficits should be incorporated in the Treaty.

Despite the emphasis on price stability, the other objectives need to be considered also: will the proposed system give the Community sufficient economic policies, both macroeconomic and microeconomic, to achieve growth, high employment and cohesion? Some argue that the Community will need a common economic policy which, because of the limited size of the Community budget, should be more *microeconomic* than *macroeconomic*.

These questions about the conduct of monetary and economic policy raise questions about the *institutional balance* in the Community. What body, on the economic side, will balance the European Central Bank's strong, and appropriate, control over monetary policy? Can the EcoFin Council become more coherent and authoritative on economic policy? Does this depend on further enhancement of the Commission's role? These issues are of importance because there are reasons to fear that the overall structure could be somewhat unbalanced — with more coherent institutions and policy on the *monetary* than on the *economic* side.

This possibility does not necessarily undermine the argument for EMU. The Community's progress has frequently involved the creation of unbalanced structures and policies, which call forth further economic and political integration. The key requirement is that the imbalance be creative rather than destructive.

An attempt was made to keep the *cohesion issue* out of the Treaty negotiations on EMU. The motivation for this was primarily political, and the analytical argument used to defend it were insufficient. The cohesion issue needs to be considered in the context of EMU because EMU will further free the economic forces which determine the regional pattern of economic activity and because economic and monetary integration greatly constrain a wide range of national policies.

The specification of the transition to EMU is an integral part of the design of the system, since it will influence the distribution of costs and benefits and the final shape of the union. These dimensions of the transition issue have given rise to debate on (i) the timing of the move to monetary union, (ii) the content of the transitional stage and (iii) a one-speed or two-speed EMU. Despite the presence of transition provisions in the new Treaty, the route to EMU remains unclear.

The main issues of concern to Ireland are the aims and scope of Community economic policy, institutional balance, cohesion and the transition to EMU.

It is important that the Irish government adopt a strategic approach to European integration, within which policy on specific matters is decided and tactical approaches devised. The outcome of the overall set of negotiations and Treaty revisions can be viewed as a *package* with four components: *money, security, institutional reform and (possible) cohesion.* From an economic perspective, the key requirement is that the Irish government's approach to *security* and *institutional reform* (and also to the parallel negotiations on CAP reform) is such as to maximise the achievement on the monetary and cohesion fronts.

The current Treaty revision is unlikely to yield sufficient progress on the political front to create a political body with the authority, capacity and legitimacy to determine a set of economic policies for the Community. This limited progress on the political front has two important implications. First, it limits the amount of progress which can be made on the cohesion issue. However, it suggests that a *further* Treaty revision could occur later in the decade and, possibly, before the Community moves to a single currency.

This reinforces some conclusions reached by NESC: (i) membership of the Community and even the existence of a Community policy, does not reduce the need for clear Irish policy aims and methods; (ii) the process of determining Community priorities occurs not only in the European Council, but also in the Commission, the Parliament and, most importantly, *in the society at large.* A perfect example of this is the priority given to the single market in recent years.

It follows that if the objective of regional convergence is to be established as a higher Community priority between now and the next Treaty revision, "it must be advocated by argument of the highest possible quality in the widest forum" (NESC, 1989). But, to date, *Ireland cannot claim to be a leader in the analysis of regional problems and the formulation of cohesion policies.*

The issue of the transition to EMU is a complex one for Ireland. Given its low inflation, and the difficulty of the existing EMS regime, there is a case for rapid movement to full EMU. There are also political arguments for this. However, a slower transition might allow time to get the economic policies, including cohesion, in place alongside the monetary provisions. But, there must be sufficient speed to keep the momentum to EMU. While it is inevitable that some countries will proceed to monetary union before others, Ireland has a definite interest in resisting certain formulations of a two-speed EMU.

1. INTRODUCTION

(i) Scope of the Paper

This paper is an overview of, and introduction to, Economic and Monetary Union (EMU). The purpose of the paper is to provide a guide to the current movement towards an economic and monetary union in the European Community. It is based on the premise that Ireland needs to consider all aspects of economic and monetary union, and not just the question of regional convergence, commonly referred to as cohesion. Consequently, this paper provides an overview and introduction to all the main issues which arise as the Community constructs a blueprint for EMU. In Section 4, I consider the relative importance of the various issues from an Irish perspective.

The paper begins with a brief account of the developments and motivations which have led the Community to advance to EMU now. As a background to the current process of Treaty revision, an explanation is provided of the limited place of monetary policy and monetary union in the existing Treaty. The definition of EMU is then discussed. A basic definition of EMU is presented and shown to be insufficient to convey the amount of policy integration which is necessary to create a genuine economic and monetary union. This is because the definition of EMU cannot be derived from purely technical economic arguments; even in defining EMU we face contentious issues about economic management and the desirable economic order of Europe. Three somewhat different recent definitions of EMU are compared and a number of issues are noted for more detailed discussion in the various papers on EMU.

Section 2 outlines a number of principles and objectives upon which agreement would seem to have been reached already and which, consequently, do not need detailed consideration. These agreed principles and objectives are: (i) parallelism between economic and monetary integration, (ii) subsidiarity and (iii) independence of the central bank and price stability as the primary objective of monetary policy.

Section 3 identifies the issues arising in the construction of EMU. Some of these have emerged as points of major disagreement at the Inter Governmental Conference (IGC); others, have received relatively little attention. Much the most significant of these issues concerns the aims and execution of overall economic policy in the Community. The likely system of economic and monetary management and the main elements of the new Treaty (as drafted by the Luxembourg Presidency) are summarised and it is shown that most arguments about the proposed structure turn on whether these Treaty provisions and certain pieces of secondary legislation, are viewed as necessary and sufficient to achieve a specified set of economic objectives. Three main perspectives are identified: one which sees completely independent monetary management as all that is necessary for monetary union; one which suggests that monetary union and price stability would be threatened unless there are binding constitutional rules on national budgetary policy; and an intermediate position which views some Community role in national budget policy as necessary for monetary union — and both inevitable and desirable for economic union.

Important issues concerning the institutional balance of the Community are then identified. The first of these highlights the possibility that the overall structure being proposed will be somewhat unbalanced — with more coherent institutions and policy on the monetary than on the economic side. Various responses to this are discussed. A second issue of institutional balance concerns the nature of central bank independence and the political and constitutional conditions in which this can be guaranteed.

An issue of some dispute is what institution will determine the external monetary or exchange rate policy of the Community. We identify some of the factors which might lie behind the different opinions on this.

Economic and monetary union will further integrate the economies of Europe and simultaneously constrain the economic policies which can be pursued by national governments. In these circumstances an important consideration is the implications of EMU for regional and social disparities. Although the question of economic and social cohesion belongs firmly in the list of issues arising in the construction of EMU, it is not considered in any detail in this introductory section. The final paper in this book is devoted to an analysis of the regional question in economic and monetary union.

Divergent perspectives on the issues of economic policy, institutional balance, EC exchange rate policy and cohesion, give rise to conflicting opinions on how the transition to EMU should be designed and accomplished. The review of the issues arising in the design and construction of EMU by considering this question. First, a thumbnail sketch is given of stages one, two and three as they are defined in the current debate at Community level. I then explain why the transition to EMU is so contentious, by identifying the issues and interests which lie behind it. Finally, these are linked to the concrete transition questions debated at the 1991 IGC: the timing of stages two and three, the content of stage two, one-speed versus two-speed EMU and the place of lagging member states and regions.

In Section 4, I identify which of these issues are of most relevance to Ireland. However, it is less important to rank the issues than to see how the issues relate to one another, and to the issues at the political union conference. Since the outcome of the overall process of negotiation and Treaty revision will be a package — encompassing money, security, institutional reform and (possibly) cohesion — it is important that the Irish government's stance on individual issues is one which is consistent with a strategic overall approach to European integration.

(ii) Background to the Current Initiative on EMU

The First Attempt to Build EMU

It can be argued that the founders of the Community expected, and intended, that it would eventually become a full economic and monetary union — though, as will be seen below — the Treaty of Rome made very little reference to monetary integration. Indeed, the current conferences to revise the Treaty are not the first time that the Community formally embarked on the road to EMU. The summit of Community leaders, meeting at The Hague in 1969, decided that the Community should create EMU. The problems in doing this, and a blueprint for its achievement, were spelled out in the famous Werner Report, the broad substance of which was adopted by the Council (now called the European Council), in 1971. Although the Community entered the first stage towards EMU — restriction on the exchange rate movements — this project was doomed to failure and was effectively shelved at the Paris summit of 1974. That attempt to move to EMU failed primarily because the member states refused to take seriously the need to coordinate their macroeconomic policies. A second reason for the failure was that the experiment unfortunately coincided with the collapse of the Bretton Woods system of international monetary management. The failure of the EMU project and, indeed, the end of the post-war golden age of growth, are widely, but mistakenly, attributed to the oil crisis of October 1973. The international monetary problem, reflecting real economic and political crises, and the failure of member states to coordinate, both antedated the oil crisis.

Why EMU Now?

The background to the current attempt to build EMU lies in the 'restarting of the Community' which occurred in the second half of the 1980s after ten years of serious malaise. That rejuvination, largely due to the first elected Parliament and the Commission which took office in 1985, led to the single market project, institutional reform and the development of new Community policies. However, even after the Single Act of 1987, the Community remained bogged down in a destructive budgetary wrangle which was not resolved until early 1988. At its meeting in Hanover in June 1988, the European Council established a Committee chaired by Mr Delors, President of the Commission, to study and propose concrete steps leading towards EMU. The committee was made up of the governors of the European central banks, in their personal capacities, and a number of independent experts. The committee submitted its report in April 1989. The current initiative on EMU can be traced to the response of member states and the Commission to the Delors Report.

To the surprise of many who had followed its deliberations from the outside, the Delors Committee reached unanimity on the need for EMU, the basic structure of the system (including control of national fiscal policy), and the main stage to the final goal. While some of the central bankers probably signed the report believing that it was primarily a descriptive document, the political implications of which would encourage Community leaders to quietly drop the idea, the Delors Report rapidly underwent a metamorphosis. It was soon seen as a prescriptive document and there followed a series of remarkable political decisions which have led to the current Treaty revision.

Three reasons can be identified for the present willingness to proceed to EMU. First, after a period of naive and dogmatic belief in general floating of exchange rates, there is now widespread disillusionment with this idea.[1] Second, the liberalisation of capital markets as part of the 1992 project, in the context of fixed exchange rates, was believed to alter the conditions for the conduct of domestic monetary policy in such a way that it required either the abandonment of fixed exchange rates or greater coordination of monetary policy. Third, the more the single market programme was processed, the more people came to believe that many of its benefits would be lost if separate currencies continued to exist.[2]

This growing interest in monetary union led the European Council to decide, in Madrid in June 1989, to proceed to EMU, starting stage one in July 1990. This may come to be seen as the most significant step towards European union since the Treaty of Rome. The Strasbourg European Council of December 1989 decided by a majority to hold an Inter Governmental Conference to draw up the Treaty revisions necessary for EMU. In Rome, in October 1990, the European Council agreed the main guidelines for the Inter Governmental Conference on EMU. These included a statement of the aims of EMU (an open market system, growth, price stability, employment, environmental protection, sound public finances and economic and social cohesion). The European Council also expressed a preference for a single currency and agreed the need for a new monetary institution, which will be 'independent' and whose primary task will be price stability. The Rome Conclusions laid down some of the procedures and conditions for moving to the final stage.[3] Eleven of the governments agreed to start stage two, including the creation of a new Community monetary institution,

---

[1]This has already been reflected in the formation of the European Monetary System (EMS), in which Ireland has participated since its inception in 1979.

[2]The Taoiseach, Mr. Haughey, has expressed support for the idea that monetary union is necessary to achieve the full potential of the single market (speech to National Management Conference, 27 April, 1991).

[3]In agreeing to the conclusions of the Rome European Council, the Taoiseach, Mr Haughey, has expressed the Irish government's support for all these principles. This in no way commits the Irish government to any particular Treaty change or concrete Community policy. No government is committed prior to its agreement to a new Treaty.

on 1 January, 1994. Finally, it was stipulated that within three years of that date the Commission and the council of the new monetary institution would report on progress, and in particular on that made in real convergence, with a view to movement to the final stage of EMU.

(iii) EMU in the Treaty of Rome

The Treaty of Rome made very little reference to monetary integration. The Treaty references to monetary integration were confined to those considered, at that time, to be necessary to achieve the Community's main concrete objective — a common market. While detailed Treaty provisions were made in respect of the customs union, the free movement of persons, services and capital, agricultural policy and competition policy, only vague reference was made to macroeconomic and monetary policy.

Article 104 set out the macroeconomic policy objectives of the EC; it is noteworthy that these objectives were described in *national* terms and it was stipulated that each *member state* shall pursue its economic policy in such a way as to ensure:

- equilibrium of its overall balance of payments
- confidence in its currency
- a high level of employment
- a stable level of prices.

While the Treaty left the core of economic policy with the member states, it did specify three ways in which the Community would achieve these four objectives. The strongest of these was the provision of Articles 105 (1) and 103, which said that member states will "coordinate their economic policies" and "regard their conjunctural policies as a matter of common concern". In addition, Article 107 (1) said that member states shall treat their exchange rate policies "as a matter of common concern". Finally, the Treaty made provision for the granting of limited credits to a member state facing serious balance of payments difficulties (Article 108).

The limited nature of the macroeconomic policy provisions of the Rome Treaty is confirmed when we note that the main institutional development to achieve coordination of monetary policies was the establishment of the advisory Monetary Committee — with a membership drawn from each government, each central bank and the Commission. The Community's role in macroeconomic and monetary policy was further constrained by the provision of Article 199 — that EC outlays and receipts must be in balance each year.

It has been argued that the caution of the Treaty in bestowing powers of monetary and economic policy on the EC can in part be explained by the economic conditions of the period: the Bretton Woods system of fixed exchange rates was functioning smoothly and the European economies were in an extended period of economic growth (Molle, 1990). Another factor may have been the prevailing perception that limited economic policy integration, and almost no macroeconomic policy integration, was necessary to achieve a common market. Such a view was strongly suggested by the prevailing theory of economic integration in which clear distinctions were made between different stages of integration, such as a custom's union, a common market and economic and monetary union. Experience since then has prompted a revision of these views of what degree of policy integration is necessary to achieve economic integration (see (iv) below).

These minor macroeconomic and monetary provisions of the Treaty were extended somewhat by the Single Act of 1987. The Single Act added a new chapter entitled 'Cooperation in Economic and Monetary Policy (Economic and Monetary Union)'. The new Chapter consists of one article which is modest in its implications. It does, however, note that "convergence of economic and monetary policies . . . is necessary for the further development of the Community" (Article 102a). But to achieve this convergence it is stipulated merely that member states "should cooperate in accordance with the objectives of Article 104" and build on the experience of EMS. It is explicitly stated that further institutional developments in the monetary area will require another revision of the Treaty.

(iv) Defining Economic and Monetary Union

It would be desirable to begin by providing a definition of economic and monetary union and only later introducing contentious issues about its desirability or the means of achieving it. Unfortunately, this is not entirely possible because the definition of EMU is itself a subject of some dispute. This is so because an important insight of the modern economics of integration is that the traditional textbook definitions of the stages of integration — free trade area, customs union, common market and economic and monetary union — are artificial and not applicable to contemporary mixed economies. One implication of this is that the distinction between a common market and an economic and monetary union loses some of its meaning, and the definition of each becomes uncertain.

We can illustrate this point, and give some idea of the meaning of EMU, by starting with a skeletal definition of EMU as involving:

- a single market for goods and services
- free movement of labour and capital

– a single currency or irreversible locking of exchange rates
– coordination of macroeconomic policies.

The value and limits of this definition of EMU can be seen if we ask what is involved in achieving each of these four requirements.

A Single Market for Goods and Services

This is a 'bare bones' definition of EMU because achievement of each of these conditions in turn requires far more than might be thought at first sight. In modern mixed economies, governments intervene in the economy in a myriad of ways, ranging from market regulation, social policy, labour market policy, industrial policy, technology policy, to direct provision of goods and service and active macroeconomic management. Many of these public policy interventions significantly affect the competitive conditions in each country. It follows that the creation of even item one above — a single market for goods and services — requires both the removal of all border interventions and some equalisation of public influences on competitive conditions in member states. But the removal of border interventions, in turn, requires harmonisation of national technical specifications and some harmonisation of indirect taxes. The equalisation of public influences on competitive conditions is very ambitious, since it implies harmonisation of sectoral regulations and sectoral aids, public aid to industry and to regions, public procurement and tendering, the deficit financing of state-owned enterprises, etc.

These insights about what is required for integration have been encapsulated in the distinction between negative and positive integration. Negative integration refers to the removal of tariffs, quotas and other national regulations and practices which are barriers to trade, investment and labour mobility. Positive integration refers to the establishment of common policies and institutions in various areas.

The analysis of what is required to establish even an single market for goods and services has two important implications for the study of EMU. First, the bare-bones definition of EMU given above is only meaningful if item one, the single market, is recognised to require not only negative integration, but also substantial positive integration. One might ask why these requirements for positive integration are not simply added to the definition of EMU given above. While this is sometimes done, it can give rise to confusion because of a second general implication of the argument outlined above.

That second implication is that, with a few exceptions (see below), there is no undisputed technical or technocratic definition of EMU. The harmonisations necessary to create a genuine single market could be achieved in a number of ways — ranging from deregulation of national interventions to reregulation and the conduct of policy by a supranational institution. Different groups, and perhaps nations, are likely to have different views on the desirable 'economic order'.[4] It follows that the necessary scope and content of Community policy — the balance of negative and positive integration — cannot be defined by reference to a technical economic theory but will, in fact, be contested by various interest groups. In his recent text, *The Economics of European Integration*, Molle makes a similar point: "policy integration will vary in extent, nature, and combination of elements of allocation, stabilisation, redistribution and external policies according to the prevailing practical political circumstances; there is no theoretical optimum blueprint for the intermediate stages between the common market and the Full Economic Union" (Molle, 1990).

Free Movement of Labour and Capital

Very similar comments apply to the second characteristic of EMU — the requirement that there be a single market for the factors of production, labour and capital, as well as for goods. This requires the development of a single labour market which, as we know, demands some approximation of a wide range of national policies in the social and labour market area. Further demanding requirements appear when financial markets are to be fully integrated. It has been argued that this would constrain domestic stabilisation and redistribution policies to such an extent that "its realisation seems to be entirely dependent on developments in macro-economic integration" (Pelkmans, 1982). In short, the creation of a genuine 'common market' seems to require the creation of economic and monetary union.

A Single Currency or Irreversible Locking of Exchange Rates

This characteristic of EMU is relatively straightforward and does derive from technical economic considerations. Of course, there remains a debate about the relative merits of retaining national currencies or establishing a single currency. This question, and many other issues concerning monetary policy, are discussed in Patrick Honohan's *Monetary Union*, the following paper in this book.[5]

Coordination of Macroeconomic Policies

Monetary union requires considerable coordination of national macroeconomic policies. Member states must pool their reserves and allow both internal and

---

[4]An economic order can be defined as a coherent set of laws, institutions and customs governing decision making in the economy and society. Although the societies of Western Europe have adopted a broadly similar economic order — the mixed economy — it is not yet clear whether the detailed relationships and institutions of the economic order are sufficiently similar, in all existing and prospective member states, for economic and political integration to be possible.

[5]The Minister of State for European Affairs, Mrs. Geoghegan-Quinn, has expressed the Irish government's preference for a single currency (speech to Magill Summer School, 12 August, 1990).

external monetary policy to be conducted by supranational institutions. This much is widely agreed and does have a clear technical basis. However, it can be argued that further coordination, or even integration, of macroeconomic policies is required if EMU is to work effectively. Others reject this view and consider that centralised and sufficiently clear conduct of monetary policy will be enough to produce a desirable macroeconomic outcome. While these arguments are partly technical, there is no universally accepted stance. Indeed, the different positions reflect not only different views on technical economic issues (such as the way the money creation process operates), but also conflicting views on political and institutional matters. The substance of these views on the coordination of macroeconomic policy is considered later in this paper, and in Patrick Honohan's paper below.

For the present, we may note that the two propositions derived above concerning item one (the single market) and item two (free movement of labour and capital) of our bare-bones definition of EMU, apply also to item three (single currency) and, especially, item four (policy coordination). First, the definition of EMU conveys only the bare bones of what is involved and it must be recognised that each item presupposes a substantial amount of positive integration. Second, nevertheless, the exact scope and content of Community policy, and balance between negative and positive integration, which is 'necessary' for EMU, cannot be defined by reference to purely economic or technocratic argument, but will, in fact, be contested by different interests.

Common Definitions of EMU

In discussions of EMU many authors do indeed explicitly include some of the additional characteristics or requirements of EMU, which we have said are implicit in our bare-bones definition. For the purposes of orienting the current debate in Ireland, it may be useful to provide three recent examples of definitions of EMU. Not surprisingly, we find that the number and type of requirements added to the bare-bones definition reflect different views on economic and political mechanisms.

The Delors Report

In setting out the principle features of EMU, the Delors Report listed separately the requirement for monetary and economic union. The Committee defined monetary union to include:

- total convertibility of currencies
- complete liberalisation of capital transactions
- irrevocable locking of exchange rates

and defined economic union in terms of four basic elements:

- the single market within which persons, goods, services and capital can move freely
- competition policy and other measures aimed at strengthening market mechanisms
- common policies aimed at structural change and regional development
- macroeconomic policy coordination, including binding rules for budgetary policies.

It can be seen that this definition includes the four elements of our bare-bones definition of EMU, adds two additional common policies (competition policy, broadly defined, and structural interventions), and specifies that the coordinated macroeconomic policy should include binding rules for budgetary policies. This reflects one particular view of what measures of positive integration are necessary to achieve genuine economic union and make complete economic and monetary union work adequately.

The European Integration Literature

In three influential texts on European integration and the one on monetary economics, we find similar definitions of EMU. Robson (1987), Swann (1988), Molle (1990) and Goodhart (1989) all add a fifth characteristic to the bare-bones definition of EMU. They say that a fifth characteristic of EMU is a degree of fiscal integration capable of providing a mechanism for inter-regional balance. This is based on various analytical and political arguments and echoes an important theme in both the current academic literature on European integration and writing on European monetary union since, at least, the mid 1960s. The arguments for including this element in the characterisation of EMU are outlined briefly in Section 3 (v) below, and are considered in greater detail in the third paper in this book, *The Regional Issue*.

The NESC Report

It may be useful to briefly report the definition of full economic and monetary union adopted by Ireland's National Economic and Social Council (NESC) in its report *Ireland in the European Community: Performance, Prospects and Strategy* (NESC, 1989). NESC defined EMU as involving:

- a completed single market with free movement of goods and factors of production (labour, financial capital and investment capital)
- an irreversible locking of exchange rates or a single currency
- Community level management of macroeconomic policy
- Community level management of a wide range of interventionist and market-regulating policies currently undertaken by the member states and,

in general, an allocation of policy functions to the Community, the member state and the local authority, based broadly on the principles of public finance.

This bears many similarities to the definition found in the literature on European integration, cited above. Recognising that a definition of EMU is partly based on a particular view of what is necessary to both achieve the union and make it work, NESC noted that this definition of EMU was adopted on the basis of:

- the modern integration literature, which stresses that national control of the wide range of market-regulating and other interventionist policies, in fact, undermines the common market by altering price signals, incentives and the mobility of labour and capital (e.g. Pelkmans, 1982)
- the theory of public finance as applied to federal structures
- the structure of existing economic and monetary unions (as reported in the MacDougall Report of 1977 and the Padoa-Schioppa Report of 1987).

The different views which underlie these slightly different perspectives on what EMU involves, reflect some of the main debates at the IGCs. Consequently, some of the differences inherent in these three definitions of EMU will recur in the debates and discussions leading up to a referendum on a new Treaty.

2. AGREED PRINCIPLES AND OBJECTIVES

Despite the existence of somewhat different views on what is necessary for EMU, a number of elements were agreed in advance and, consequently, were not contested at the 1991 IGC. These are reported here and briefly explained, since they are frequently cited in current discussion.

(i) Parallelism

In the Delors Report, it was argued strongly that economic union and monetary union form "the two integral parts of a single whole and would therefore have to be implemented in parallel" (paragraph 21). As a result, in setting out the "principles governing a step-by-step approach" to EMU, the Delors Committee included "parallelism" among these. This has since been ratified by the European Council, at Madrid in June 1989, and must be viewed as one of the principles upon which the new Treaty, and any action flowing from it, are based. The Irish government has laid great stress on this principle.[6]

However, three things must be noted about the principle of parallelism. First, as noted in the Delors Report, perfect parallelism between progress on the economic and monetary fronts is not possible. Indeed, in the words of the Delors Committee, "Some temporary deviations from parallelism are part of the dynamic process of the Community". However, the Delors Committee was quite clear that, given the degree of monetary coordination already achieved, "material progress on the economic policy front would be necessary for further progress on the monetary policy front" (paragraph 42). Second, it is clear from this that the principle of parallelism is related to the idea of 'convergence' in that economic convergence is widely considered to be a precondition for monetary union. Progress to monetary union without sufficient prior convergence of the European economies could be considered to violate the principle of parallelism. Third, parallelism, like convergence, is open to various interpretations.[7] Adherence to a broad or narrow interpretation of parallelism largely depends on whether one considers that a greater or lesser amount of economic policy should be conducted at Community level.[8]

---

[6]See the statements by the Taoiseach, Mr. Haughey, on recent European Council meetings (Dail Eireann, 13 December, 1989, and 9 July, 1991). The Minister for Finance, Mr. Reynolds, laid emphasis on parallelism in his address to the Committee on Economic and Monetary Affairs of the European Parliament (28 February, 1990). The Governor of the Central Bank, Mr. Doyle, has also stressed the need for parallel progress on economic and monetary integration (address to the Irish Council of the European Movement, Galway, 17 April, 1991).

[7]The word convergence generally refers to what would more accurately be described as 'nominal convergence' — convergency of inflation rates, interest rates and budget deficits. The word cohesion refers to what might be called 'real convergence' — the convergence of income levels and unemployment rates.

[8]The Taoiseach, Mr Haughey, has suggested that parallelism should imply, among other things, specific Community action to promote cohesion in the context of moves to the second and third stages of EMU (speech to National Management Conference, 27 April, 1991).

(ii) Subsidiarity

Economic and monetary union inevitably involves further transfers of decision-making power from member states to the Community as a whole. The extent of such a transfer, and the method for the exercise of power at the Community level, are among the central questions in the current debate on EMU and discussed in this book. Whatever economic arguments are introduced on this subject, the Delors Report laid considerable stress on the 'principle of subsidiarity' (paragraph 20). The principle is that policy functions should be undertaken at the lowest level of government which can undertake them effectively and efficiently.

The principle of subsidiarity was among those laid down at the Madrid European Council in June 1989. The principle was included in the Draft Treaties prepared by both the Commission and the Luxembourg Presidency. The idea is that the principle of subsidiarity be included in the early articles of the Treaty — which define the objectives of the Community and the means by which they are to be achieved.

While this aspect of the treaty is primarily an issue in discussions on political union, it is clearly of potential significance to EMU, and especially economic union. However, there is no doubt that subsidiarity means different things to different people. While many would consider that the concept is currently used to limit the scope of Community policy, some in Britain believe that the European institutions themselves see subsidiarity as a vehicle for furthering political union and enhancing their powers. However, this view, that 'subsidiarity could well become a federalist Trojan horse' is not shared in other Community countries.

Although subsidiarity is one of the principles agreed earlier by the member states, three fundamental aspects of it remain contentious. First, what is the place and status of subsidiarity in the new Treaty? Second, will the principle be legally judiciable? Third, and most important, how will it be interpreted? The last is the most important question because the principle can only be applied, or abused, when criteria are set out for deciding when a policy is being 'conducted effectively' at the local or national level or, to use the language of the Delors Report, conducted "without adverse repercussions on the cohesion and functioning of the economic and monetary union" (Delors Report, paragraph 20). To make the notion of subsidiarity meaningful, these criteria would require to be based on some coherent economic or political doctrine.[9]

[9]Although the Irish government supported the statement on subsidiarity at the Madrid European Council, it clearly has some reservations about this idea. The Minister of State for European Affairs, Mrs Geoghegan-Quinn, has expressed the government's concern that the principle of subsidiarity should not be applied in any unduly restrictive way, so as to hamstring the assignment of necessary policy functions to the Community. She has suggested that the principle should not be made any more explicit in the Treaty and that its interpretation and application should be undertaken at the political rather than the judicial level (speech to Magill Summer School, 12 August, 1990).

(iii) Price Stability and Central Bank Independence

Although there are undoubtedly different national approaches to both the priority of price stability and the independence of central banks, it is safe to say that if there is to be a European monetary union it will be based on a treaty which incorporates these principles. This is so, if only because Germany will not agree to monetary union on any other terms.

Price Stability in the Treaty

In its Draft Treaty, the Luxembourg Presidency proposed that Article 3 should include among the activities of the Community:

> 3a (2) the introduction of a single currency, the ecu, the definition and conduct of a single monetary and exchange rate policy, the over-riding objective of which should be to maintain price stability and, without prejudice to this objective, to support the general economic policy of the Community, in a manner compatible with free and competitive market principles.

This definition of price stability as the primary objective of monetary policy was also advocated by the Delors Committee and in addition is incorporated in the draft Statutes of the European System of Central Banks as drawn up by the central bank governors.[10]

This approach is reflected in the institutional provisions of the proposed new Treaty. Article 4, and a proposed Article 4a, which define the institutions of the Community, distinguish between the four existing institutions (European Parliament, the Council, the Commission and the Court of Justice), and the new central bank because, unlike these bodies, the central bank will have a legal personality of its own and will not be subject to the administrative and financial rules laid down in the existing Treaty. More significantly, Articles 104, 106, 107 and 108 guarantee the bank's independence by outlawing any influence by the Community or member states on any central bank "in the peformance of its tasks", by outlawing central bank loans or credit facilities to any public body, and by specifying that the Executive Board of the bank will be appointed (by the Council), for a period of eight years.

The provisions defining the independence of the central bank are closely modelled on Article 157 (2) of the earlier EEC Treaty, which establishes the independence of members of the European Commission.

---

[10]The Governor of the Central Bank, Mr. Doyle, has outlined the arguments for an independent European Central Bank (address to Business International Roundtable, 18 June, 1991). An Irish government official has defended the idea of price stability as the major objective of monetary policy: "the emphasis on low inflation may at times have a disinflationary effect that will, in the short term, run counter to our efforts to promote growth and employment. In the longer term a stable economic environment with low inflation will be an essential precondition for steady growth and more employment" ('Irish Attitude to EMU and the Irish Conditions for Entry', speech by Mr. Maurice O'Connell, Department of Finance, Conrad Hotel, Dublin, 21 March, 1991).

Economic and Political Substance

Although we can identify central bank independence and the priority of price stability (in monetary policy) as among the principles and objectives agreed before the 1991 IGC, and as inevitable in any EMU Treaty, these principles and the Treaty articles expressing them do not foreclose all discussion. This is because the economic and political substance of the new regime is not fully determined by the Treaty articles outlined above. It follows, that despite the acceptance of these principles there are many substantive issues of economic and monetary management to be discussed below and in the later chapters of the book (see also the papers in the series, *Studies in European Union: Political Union,* IEA, 1991). These substantive economic and political issues include the aims of Community exchange rate policy and the political conditions for central bank independence.

3. ISSUES ARISING IN THE CONSTRUCTION OF EMU

This section identifies the main issues which arise in the construction of a European economic and monetary union. No attempt is made to provide an evaluation of the various arguments which can be heard on each issue. One purpose here is to alert the reader to the key issues at the 1991 Inter Governmental Conference on EMU and to explain how these are addressed, or not addressed, in a new Treaty. Five main issues can be identified: first, the aims and execution of economic policy; second, and closely related to the first, a new institutional balance; third, external monetary policy or Community exchange rate policy; fourth, economic and social cohesion in the union; and, fifth, the transition to EMU.

(i) The Aims and Execution of Economic Policy

It has been seen in Section 1 that only a small part of the integration process can be identified by reference to technical economic criteria — the greater part of what is included in, or excluded from, integration being contested by various arguments and interests. This is true of the core economic areas of monetary policy, fiscal policy, redistributive policy and industrial policy. Integration proceeds at a different pace in each of these areas and this alters the significance of the policies which remain under national control.

The Proposed System and Treaty Revisions

Rather than rehearse the various arguments about the desirable combination of monetary, fiscal and microeconomic policy, it may be best to summarise the likely structure and then to identify the main interpretations of it. In describing the likely system of economic and monetary union, I draw primarily on the new Treaty as drafted by the Luxembourg Presidency mid-way through the 1991 Inter Governmental Conference on EMU. However, since this new Draft Treaty is conservative, in the sense that it seeks to change the existing Treaty as little as possible, its provisions do not convey an adequate picture of the likely system. Consequently, in summarising EMU reference is made to secondary legislation which exists or is likely to be enacted.

As economic policy *objectives* of the Community, the new Draft Treaty proposes:

- growth
- a high level of employment
- price stability
- convergence of economic performance
- economic and social cohesion.[11]

[11]In addition to these Community 'objectives', 'sound public finances' and 'a healthy balance of payments' are stated as 'guiding principles' in Article 3a of the Draft Treaty. By contrast, the Commission listed these among the objectives of policy in its Draft Treaty. The Irish government has proposed that *full* employment should be among the objectives stated in Article 2.

The *instruments* proposed to achieve the main economic goals are a common monetary policy plus:

- multinational surveillance of economic developments in the Community (Article 103)
- multiannual economic policy guidelines to member states (Article 103a) and secondary legislation
- Community financial assistance to a member state seriously threatened with difficulties (Article 103).

Three *budgetary rules* are also specified:

- no monetary financing (Article 104)
- no bailing out of member states (Article 104)
- no excessive deficits (Article 104).

Reasons for Conflicting Positions

Most argument about this Treaty and legislative structure turns on whether the provisions summarised above are viewed as both necessary and sufficient to achieve the five objectives outlined in Article 2a. It should be noted that opinions differ on this for four sorts of reasons: conflicting theories on how the economy works; different views on the way governments, states and Community institutions work; different interpretations of what the policy instruments and rules outlined above mean; and, it has to be said, attachment of different priorities to each of the five objectives. It is not always possible, or necessary, to say which of these four reasons underlies a given difference of opinion. But it is, nevertheless, important to recognise the four dimensions to the argument; for example, without this recognition one could conduct a fruitless search to trace a dispute to some fundamental difference in economic doctrine when, in reality, it is based on a difference of opinion on how Community or national institutions are likely to work or on a difference of policy priorities.

Monetary Policy and Fiscal Rules

One of the central issues in the design of EMU is the degree to which monetary union requires Community control of national fiscal policies. This has been a major subject of debate in the Community and is one of the key issues in formal negotiations on the constitutional and legal foundation of EMU. In order to provide an introduction to somewhat complex arguments, we identify and explain three contrasting viewpoints on this question.

One position is that many of the provisions outlined above are not necessary in order to achieve monetary union and its chief objective, price stability. This view, which I refer to as the minimalist monetary perspective, sees the establishment of an independent central bank and a firm commitment to no bailing out of any government as the necessary and sufficient conditions for EMU with price stability. The proposed rule against monetary financing of public deficits is not included in this specification mainly because it is taken as implicit in the definition of a Central Bank which is completely independent of government in every way. A definite implication of this viewpoint is that there is certainly no need for Community control of national budget deficits.

There are arguments in favour of this minimalist monetary perspective. The rejection of the proposed Community control of national budgetary policy may be supported by the argument that the need to finance any national budget deficit by sale of debt, as a result of no provision of central bank finance, means that the financial markets will automatically discipline governments by means of price and quantity constraints reflecting market evaluation. In addition, proponents of this view would be inclined to be sceptical of the possibility of Community control, pointing to the fact that two of the proposed 'instruments' — multiannual guidelines and multilateral surveillance — exist already and do not work, in that they achieve very little coordination of macroeconomic policies. Given the perspective in question this failure of economic policy coordination is not viewed as a threat to monetary union and price stability. This is not to dismiss the argument that greater coordination is needed for successful economic integration — and the adherents to the minimalist monetary perspective may well accept the view that the interdependence of the European economies implies that better macroeconomic results could be achieved from coordinated policies.

A polar opposite view can also be identified, according to which monetary union and price stability would be threatened unless there were binding constitutional rules limiting national budgetary deficits. This case is built up from the observation that fiscal policy is frequently a major determinant of monetary growth. One argument in support of this case is the view that financial markets provide insufficient discipline and, to the extent that they do, they tend to create abrupt closures of access to market financing. The case for binding constitutional limits on deficit spending requires the additional argument that such rules can be enforced in a meaningful way. It is not obvious that constitutional balanced budget provisions have any meaning or effect other than as an encouragement to creative accounting.

A case for binding treaty rules on budgetary policies was made by the Delors Committee. However, it is important to note that the argument in the Delors Report was not simply that such rules are a technical necessity for the existence of monetary union and the maintenance of price stability (the argument which is rejected by the minimalist monetary perspective considered above). Much of the Delors Committee's argument for Community control of national budgetary policies was based on the view that close budgetary coordination was also necessary if the economic union was to achieve the other goals listed above, i.e. growth and a high level of employment.

It is possible to identify an intermediate position, between the two polar views outlined above. This view would tend to see most of the proposed treaty provisions and secondary legislation as necessary and sufficient for monetary union and price stability, and as possibly sufficient for achievement of the other economic policy goals.

Where monetary union and price stability are concerned this intermediate position differs from the minimalist monetary position more on institutional grounds than on grounds of economic theory. First, it could be argued that some Community control of budget deficits, and instruments to coordinate policy, are warranted because, political realities being what they are, there cannot be a binding treaty provision against bail outs. Indeed, it is of interest that the proposed Treaty article does not say 'no bail outs', but that the Community shall not be liable for the commitments of member states or public authorities (Article 104). Second, there may be a conflict between the 'no bail out' provision (such as it is) and the new financial assistance mechanism proposed to replace the earlier balance of payments assistance provision of Article 108 (EEC). But it can be argued that it would be impossible to attract states into a monetary system which did not include any provision for financial support in the event of severe pressure; but if the financial support clause is an unavoidable feature of the system, then some Community control of national policy is equally necessary — if only to ensure that the support mechanism is rarely used.

This reading of the political processes within the Community suggests that there is a need for a set of provisions of the sort that has been proposed by the Commission and various member states and embodied in the new Treaty (as drafted by the Luxembourg Presidency). In saying this it cannot be denied that the proposed provisions are both partly contradictory and partly unclear. The intermediate viewpoint is one which suggests that the apparent contradictions and the definite obscurities can only be clarified in practice. For example, it could be argued that the following important questions will only be answered when the Community moves to a new system: What does 'excessive budget deficits' mean? In the event that an excessive budget deficit is deemed to have arisen, what sanctions will exist in the 'multiannual guidelines' and 'multilateral surveillance'? How will these methods of policy coordination be made effective in the EcoFin Council? If Article 104 (1a) does not really mean 'no bail out', what criteria will be applied in practice and what conditionality enforced?

The essence of this argument is that a somewhat messy constitution, which will only take shape in practice, will ultimately be more robust and more effective, *even for achieving price stability,* than a more austere, minimal, and perhaps logical, constitution. The fear would be that a system based purely on complete central bank independence, plus no bailing out, would be hard on inflation, for sure, but would be brittle. It would inevitably come under pressure, either because unsustainable borrowing was in fact funded by the financial markets or, more generally, because other economic goals, such as growth or employment, were not achieved. The arrangement would be brittle because, although such pressure would initially be completely resisted, given the design of the system, it would be likely to succeed eventually — at which point the independence of the monetary authority could jump from being total to being non-existent. In other words, we may face a choice between a regime which is totally anti-inflation most of the time, and a regime which is probably anti-inflation all of the time.

This intermediate view, that considerable Community control of budget deficits and considerable coordination of fiscal policy, are desirable to make monetary union work, is reinforced when economic union and economic objectives are considered. For example, if economic union implies considerable legal and market pressure for harmonisation of tax systems, then the Community is automatically drawn into the area of national fiscal policy (for a discussion of implications of economic integration for national fiscal systems see NESC, 1989, Chapter 12).

Consideration of economic policy goals may also suggest that some Community involvement in national fiscal policy should be considered. The Delors Committee advanced the following argument:

> the fact that the centrally-managed Community budget is likely to remain a very small part of total public sector spending and that much of this budget will not be available for cyclical adjustments will mean that the task of setting a Community-wide fiscal policy stance will have to be performed through the coordination of national budgetary policies. Without such coordination it would be impossible for the Community as a whole to establish a fiscal-monetary policy mix appropriate for the preservation of internal balance, or for the Community to play its part in the international adjustment process (Delors Report, paragraph 30).

Indeed it can be argued that the potential inflationary or recessionary consequences of the budgetary stance in one member country will be increasingly important to its neighbours and to the Community as EMU proceeds. This suggests that, in certain circumstances, budgetary policy should be used to correct macroeconomic disturbances. For this to work, the EcoFin Council would have to define an appropriate budgetary stance for the Community as a whole and — as long as the Community budget is, as at present, of minor importance in this context — take a view on the extent to which national budgetary stances are consistent with it. Indeed, the Community's analysis might usefully cover not only deficits and surpluses but also the structures of revenue and expenditure. As well as lending support to the idea of Community involvement in fiscal policy, this line of thought raises important questions concerning the institutional balance in the Community, to which we now turn.

(ii) Institutional Balance

One of the most important requirements in the design of EMU is to find an institutional structure which is capable of formulating and executing the necessary economic and monetary policies. While this may seem obvious, it needs to be emphasised because recent public discussion of the institutional requirements of EMU has tended to focus on the monetary side, to the possible neglect of economic policy. This neglect of the need for a common economic policy, and of the relevant institutions probably reflects the particular sensitivities of a few governments and the tendency of all national governments and administrations to resist Community involvement in new policy areas. However, this nationalism cannot completely conceal the underlying economic realities and it is not surprising, therefore, that despite the best efforts of governments, the question of a common economic policy and its institutional requirements forced its way on to the agenda to some degree. In this section, I outline some of the factors which need to be considered when thinking about the two main institutional issues.

The first of these is the institutional requirements for the formation of the common economic policy. The second is the institutional requirements and implications of central bank 'independence'. One other issue of some importance at the IGC — the setting of exchange rate policy — has a significant institutional dimension, but this is discussed in a separate section below.

The Common Economic Policy

Does the creation of EMU require institutional developments to facilitate the formulation and implementation of a common economic policy? To discuss this question it is necessary to decide first, whether, and to what extent, the Community requires a common economic policy.

There are two broad dimensions to the common economic policy which the Community might develop: on the one hand macroeconomic policy; and, on the other, a range of policies which might be called *microeconomic*.

We have noted arguments for various degrees of Community involvement in the fiscal policy of member states ranging from non involvement, through sufficient control to avert deficits which might disrupt monetary policy and price stability, to definition of an appropriate budgetary stance for the Community as a whole. If either the second or third of these three positions was accepted, and this seems very likely, then the question arises — will the Community be capable of formulating and implementing a common fiscal policy?

In addition, a strong case can be made for Community involvement in a wide range of microeconomic policies — such as industrial policy, technology policy, transport policy, energy policy, manpower policy, social policy, regional policy and taxation policy.

Indeed, it can be argued that the Community economic policy — which will be necessary if the objectives of growth, employment, balance of payments equilibrium and cohesion are to be achieved — should be more *microeconomic* than *macroeconomic*. But, as in the case of macroeconomic policy, there may also be an institutional problem to be overcome, since the Council may not yet possess the effectiveness or legitimacy to develop such policies.

On the question of the need for a 'common economic policy', and the related institutional issues, we can discern a contrast between the view of the Commission and the view implicit in the new Treaty (as drafted by the Luxembourg Presidency).

In its Draft Treaty, submitted at the start of the Inter Governmental Conferences on political union and EMU, the Commission suggested that alongside the single monetary policy, the Community should have "a common economic policy based on the definition of common objectives" and that this should be included among the activities of the Community listed in Article 3 of the Treaty. In its Explanatory Memorandum, the Commission stresses that, in the context of independent monetary policy and very limited national budget deficits, the field of common economic policy must be much wider than monetary policy and Community guidelines concerning national budget deficits. These can achieve one of the Community's economic policy objectives — price stability — but the Community will need other policies if it is to achieve its other economic objectives: growth, high employment, balance of international payments, and cohesion.

This view that the Community needs a wide ranging 'common economic policy' was reflected in the institutional arrangements implicit and explicit in the Commission's Draft Treaty. In the emerging economic policy areas the Commission defined arrangements between the European Council, the EcoFin Council, the Commission and the Parliament which could alter the existing institutional pattern. In proposing a Treaty basis for three of the evolving economic policy instruments — multiannual guidelines, specific recommendations to each member state, and multilateral surveillance — the Commission suggested that it should be the institutional centre of the process of economic analysis and policy proposal, with the Council retaining the ultimate power of decision. For example, the Commission draft suggested a direct relationship between the Commission and member states concerning the implementation of policy recommendations decided by the Council. Most significantly, in defining the institutional provisions for the conduct of monetary policy the Commission draft envisaged a direct relationship between itself and the European Central Bank, including observations by the Commission which "have a bearing on the consistency between economic and monetary policy", and which may be published. Although the Commission defended some of these roles on the grounds that they would enhance democratic accountability — since the Commission is accountable to Parliament — one senses that the underlying motivation was to secure the Community's capacity to act in the economic sphere.

The economic policy provisions and institutional relationships implicit and explicit in the new Treaty (as drafted by the Luxembourg Presidency) differ somewhat from those described above. All explicit reference to a 'common economic policy' has disappeared. The fundamental activities of the Community include merely "the adoption, within a framework of a system of markets which are competitive and open both internally and externally, of an economic policy *based on the close coordination of the member states' economic policies*" (Article 3a, emphasis added). The main article which defines economic policy repeats the Rome Treaty provision that "*member states shall conduct their economic policy with a view to contributing* to the achievement of the objectives of economic and monetary union" (Article 102a, emphasis added). However, Article 103 does stipulate that: "After discussion in the European Council, the Council, acting by a qualified majority on a proposal from the Commission, shall define the broad outlines of the economic policy of the Community and of its member states".

This more limited view of the role of Community economic policy in EMU is, to some extent, reflected in the institutional provisions in the new Treaty. These put less emphasis on the Commission and more on the Council but, in doing so, occasionally leave the reader unclear about what institution will do what. For example, the process of economic monitoring by the Council will "include the forwarding of details by Member States of any important measure to be taken in the field of their economic policy" (Article 103). But it is not clear to what institution these details will be forwarded. One institutional proposal in the new Treaty which may turn out to be significant is the provision for creation of a new 'economic and financial committee' (Article 109b). While this is formally a replacement of the existing Monetary Committee (defined in Article 105 of the Treaty of Rome), the text suggests that its remit is to be extended, to include economic matters, and its role enhanced. For example, it is explicitly assigned the role of preparing the work of the Council in the two key economic policy areas of multilateral surveillance and avoidance of excessive deficits (Articles 103 and 104a). The existing Monetary Committee, and the proposed replacement, is essentially a Council body — being composed of representatives from each member state and from the Commission, and reporting to the Council. The fear must be entertained that the Council will not have the capacity to formulate and agree a sufficiently clear economic policy, and that the preparation of its expanding workload by another Council body will perpetuate, rather than transcend, the proven limits of intergovernmentalism.

The Elements of the Institutional Issue

The purpose of this discussion is not to draw a contrast between the Commission and the Council — in the sense that the former wants a 'strong'

Commission and the latter a 'strong' Council. For those who see a need for common policies, the issue is not the balance of power between the Commission and the Council, but the balance between the *Community institutions* (the Commission and Council together) and the *member states,* and between the Community institutions and the central bank. In the end, the institutional issue concerns the capacity of the Council — since this is the body which would have to make decisions. But the institutional issue arises precisely because of the poor record of either the European Council or the EcoFin Council in coordinating macroeconomic policies, let alone formulating a common policy. Furthermore, of the main economic policy instruments which are being put in the Treaty to enhance the coordination of macroeconomic policy, several — including multilateral surveillance (Article 103) and economic policy recommendations (Article 103a) — exist already and have not noticeably improved policy coordination.

The question is how can the capacity of the Council be enhanced? This is not the same as enhancing the powers of the Council, because a strong Council can mean a weak Community institution.[12] It seems to be agreed that the existing institutional balance cannot survive. One argument is that to enhance the capacity of the Council requires not only further extension of majority voting, etc., but also deeper involvement of the Commission in the economic policy area.

This approach contrasts with the kind of 'strengthening' of the Council which could, in some circumstances, result from a Treaty revision which did not take adequate account of the fact that the existing institutional balance will inevitably be changed (by the creation of a new Community institution — the European Central Bank) and which thereby failed to explicitly design an institutional structure for economic policy making. It would be unfortunate if, at the same time as Community involvement in economic policy is extended somewhat (to include, for example, national budget deficits), that involvement simultaneously became more intergovernmental and less supranational. This could result in wider Community involvement but no greater Community capacity. If there is validity in the argument that the underlying economic reality requires a common economic policy, then this lack of capacity would, in general, lead to a poorer economic performance and could, in certain circumstances, be the cause of an economic catastrophe.

While it is too early to be certain, there are reasons to fear that the overall structure being proposed could be somewhat unbalanced — with more coherent institutions and policy on the monetary than the economic side. While this might lead some to approach the proposed EMU with extreme caution, a number of other reactions are possible, and I discuss some of these now.

---

[12]To see this, consider the question: are current Councils, for example, the Council of Agriculture Ministers, weak or strong.

The first qualification is that the actual institutional balance, and the coherence of economic policy, depends as much on those involved, and how they behave, as on the constitutional definition of their powers and relationships. Indeed, while it is possible to lay down constitutional rules for the conduct of a monetary authority and its relations with other bodies (and even this possibility can be exaggerated, as will be seen below), it would be difficult to define such rules or procedures for the conduct of economic policy.

Furthermore, it is possible to recognise that the proposed system is unbalanced, with a potential vacuum on the economic policy side, but to place one's faith in the fact that the 'Community method' consists precisely in proceeding in an unbalanced way and relying on the 'integrative logic', which dictates that the achievement of one stage of integration will necessarily force on to the agenda the consideration of further integration. An example of this thinking can be found in the Commission's recent document *One Market, One Money,* where it is argued that the EcoFin will be forced, by the existence of EuroFed, to evolve into the "political and decision making authority on the economic side" which the Monetary Committee, and many others, recognise to be necessary. Indeed, the Commission itself constitutes a prime example of these points. The history of the Community shows that a dynamic Commission can advance integration within the existing institutional structure and, thereby, overcome the inherent limits of the intergovernmental element in the Community's constitutional structures.

If this general argument in defence of unbalanced progress were accepted, certain specific considerations can be added to it. The decade of the eighties has been one in which monetary and inflation concerns have dominated economic policy to a remarkable degree. It can be argued that this widespread, but ultimately unsustainable, dominance of monetary issues creates an opportunity for a further step in European integration which should be grasped. A similar argument can be made about the particular political conjuncture which exists —with Germany willing to proceed in a way which might not happen again. Furthermore, where 'political union' was once seen as a defineable point or degree of political integration it has, during the current phase, been transformed into a *process.* Since economic and monetary union is profoundly political, we may thus have no choice but to conceive of it as a process also — though the strictly *monetary* element does not easily lend itself to this approach. Our discussion of the definition and content of EMU suggests that this transformation of EMU into a process, though it parallels developments on the political side, will not be economically and socially neutral — in the sense that it will create one kind of EMU rather than another.

However, if these considerations suggest support for progress to EMU, despite the unbalanced structure which may emerge, they do, nevertheless, raise immediate issues about the new Treaty. How can it be guaranteed that the imbalance is creative rather than destructive? Can the Treaty be revised in such a way as to facilitate, or enable, the development of the effective and legitimate political authority which is necessary to determine the economic policy of the Community? Can this be done in such a way as to avoid the need for further Treaty revisions in a few years time? These are genuine concerns because the history of the Community lends only partial support to the theory that the 'integrative logic' necessarily propels the Community forward. Indeed, systematic tendencies to minimum Community intervention and even blockages to integration have also been identified (Pelkmans, 1982; Pinder, 1987).

Central Bank Independence

A particular instance of the question of institutional balance arises when we consider the independence of the European Central Bank. Although this question is discussed in detail by Patrick Honohan, in his paper on the monetary dimension, it may be helpful to the reader if I briefly consider the relationship between central bank independence and constitutional design here. This will allow us to place the question of central bank independence in the context of the current review of the overall institutional and political balance of the Community. In its recent report, *A Strategy for the Nineties: Economic Stability and Structural Change*, NESC draws attention to some of the possible institutional and constitutional requirements for the independence of a European Central Bank. NESC suggests that the independence of a central bank can only be defined with reference to actual systems of government. The U.S. Federal Reserve and the German Bundesbank are widely considered to be among the most independent central banks, and this suggests that these cases are worth studying.

Such a study gives some indication of what independence is *not*, as well as what it is. First, an independent central bank does not seem to mean a central bank that has an over-riding legal duty to prevent inflation. The legal duties of both the Bundesbank and the Fed include the objectives of growth and employment as well as price stability. "The result of these provisions is that the Bundesbank and the Fed are not legally constrained to adopt any particular monetary policy nor to give priority to anti-inflationary goals at the expense of other economic objectives" (Harden, 1990).

Second, the independence of a central bank does not seem to derive primarily from its legal status. In the case of the US, there is no constitutional or legislative provision guaranteeing the independence of the Fed. In the case of Germany, the extent to which constitutional law guarantees the independence of the Bundesbank is a matter of debate (Harden, 1990).

Third, the independence of the Fed and the Bundesbank would seem to derive from the fact that they are political actors within a political and constitutional system which gives them some power against other actors — especially other parts of government. The reason for this differs in the cases of the US and

Germany, reflecting historical factors. Putting these different origins aside the position can be summarised as follows:

> For a central bank 'independence' is thus a matter of degree. It means not that the bank pursues its own policies regardless of what anyone else is doing, but that as an institution it has the power to make its own political choices about which policies it will pursue. Such power is only partly dependent on specific legal provisions. Furthermore, it is neither unlimited nor irrevocable. Ultimately if a central bank is to remain an autonomous political actor its role must be accepted as legitimate. That is, it must not just exercise power but also be generally acknowledged as possessing the constitutional right to do so (Harden, 1990).

It is clear, therefore, that the independence of a central bank depends on its legitimacy, which in turn depends on the constitution within which it functions.

NESC considers that, if this is the true nature and source of the independence of the US Fed and the Bundesbank, then the independence of the European Central Bank can be assisted, but not guaranteed, by its formal objectives, its legal status and its method of appointment and voting. In practice, its independence and accountability will depend on the overall constitutional and political constellation within which it will be an important body. This point has been well put as follows:

> Whether it will be possible for the EuroFed to achieve legitimacy as a political actor depends on who the other actors are and on the constitutional framework in which they operate. This means that the legitimacy of the EuroFed cannot be considered simply in relation to monetary union; it depends on the broader constitutional framework of the Community. In particular, it depends on the allocation of power over economic policy, both as between different Community institutions and as between those institutions and member states. In other words, from a constitutional perspective, monetary union cannot be sensibly examined except in the context of economic union . . . It is important that between the details of monetary union and the aspirations of political union, the constitutional framework of *economic* union should also be tackled (Harden, 1990).

This emphasis on the constitutional framework is of the utmost importance and suggests that the minimalist position outlined at the beginning of this paper — according to which legal independence and a constitutional ban on bailing out are all that are required for monetary union — is not really a replication at the European level of German or US systems and, in fact, constitutes a proposal to devise a novel system.

In reply to this it can be argued that, for various reasons, the Community cannot replicate the German or US systems and will, perforce, be inventing a new system. Indeed in this vein, it could be said that, precisely because the political consensus or balance which underlies the German and US system *does not exist in the Community,* then it is necessary to have a monetary union which is completely held down by constitutional provisions and is not reliant in any way on political processes.

(iii) EC Exchange Rate Policy

One issue which has emerged as significant at the IGC is the question of what institution is to determine the external monetary or exchange rate policy of the Community.

It would probably not be disputed, that the Council must have the power to decide on major changes of exchange rate regime, such as the establishment of a new Bretton Woods type arrangement. It is equally clear that the Bank must be free to conduct day-to-day monetary policy, and must decide on the timing and amount of intervention in the money market. However, the fact that this issue continues to be contentious at the IGC, if we are to believe reports, suggest that there is some disagreement about who determines policy between these parameters.

This is strongly reflected in the new Treaty (as drafted by the Luxembourg Presidency). It is clear that the Council will be the final arbiter of the exchange rate system of the Community "including, in particular, the adoption, adjustment and abandoning of central rates *vis-a-vis* third currencies" (Article 109). Whether these decisions will be made by qualified majority or unanimity is not yet resolved. Furthermore, in place of the normal procedure of proposal from the Commission, it is suggested that the Council can act on a proposal from a member state or the Central Bank. Finally, it is stipulated that the Council will consult with the Bank "in an endeavour to reach consensus".

Given the close connection between internal monetary policy and the external value of the ecu (see Patrick Honohan's *Monetary Union,* the following paper in this book), it is possible that disagreement on exchange rate policy is, in fact, quite substantial. With all parties agreeing, or perhaps paying lip service, to the big principles of independence and no monetary financing, fundamental disagreements about monetary policy may be finding expression through this issue of Community exchange rate policy. If this is the case then many of the issues discussed above, concerning both the basic design of EMU and the new institutional balance, are relevant to this question of exchange rate policy and it is not the narrow technical question which it may seem at first sight.

(iv) Cohesion: Regional and Social Convergence

Economic and monetary union will further integrate the economies of Europe and simultaneously constrain the economic policies which can be pursued by national governments. In these circumstances an important consideration is the implication of EMU for regional and social disparities. This will depend, in part, on the economic effects of moving to EMU and the economic laws which will prevail in such a union. The extent of regional and social inequalities will also depend on policy at both Community and national level, and how these are changed in the construction of EMU.

Although the question of cohesion belongs firmly in the list of issues arising in the construction of EMU, it is not considered in this introductory chapter. The final paper in this book is devoted to an analysis of the regional question in economic and monetary union. In that paper I discuss the place of the cohesion issue in the recent negotiations on EMU and offer a perspective on the place of the cohesion question in the Community system. The likely regional pattern of economic activity and income in a European economic and monetary union is considered and the relative significance of monetary and real factors is assessed. Finally, the issues arising for both Ireland and the Community are identified and analysed.

(v) The Transition to EMU

Divergent perspectives on all of these issues — the aims and execution of economic policy, institutional balance, EC exchange rate policy and cohesion — give rise to conflicting opinions on how the transition to EMU should be designed and accomplished. Furthermore, independent of divergent perspectives on these issues, the question of transition to EMU is a significant one in its own right. For these reasons, the question of transition to EMU was one of the important contested issues at the 1991 IGC.

Outline of Stages One, Two and Three

In order to discuss this it is first necessary to provide a brief outline of the stages of EMU as they are currently defined in the Community. These definitions derive from the Delors Committee's report on EMU.

Stage one was defined as a preparatory stage. On the economic side it would include the completion of the single market, the reduction of regional disparities and the development of new procedures for coordination of member states' economic and fiscal policies. On the monetary side, there would be the creation of a single financial area and all Community countries would become members of the EMS. The mandate of the existing Committee of Central Bank Governors would be extended to strengthen its monitoring of monetary and exchange rate policy in the Community and it would express opinions to individual governments on their conduct of policy. Stage one also involves the revision of the Treaty in order to establish the legal basis for full EMU.

Stage two could begin when the new Treaty comes into force. It was defined by the Delors Committee as a phase of institutional development. In the economic field the performance of structural and regional policies would be evaluated and, if necessary, adapted and strengthened. The procedures and content of macroeconomic coordination would be further developed to include adoption of policy guidelines by majority decision. During this stage, Community rules on, for example, budget deficits would not be legally binding. The main institutional development would be the establishment of the European System of Central Banks (ESCB), comprising the national central banks and a European body. The ESCB would develop the ability to formulate and implement a single monetary policy, but the ultimate responsibility for monetary policy decisions would remain with national authorities.

The third and final stage of EMU would begin with the irrevocable locking of exchange rates. In the economic field, stage three would involve a move to binding Community rules on macroeconomic and budgetary policy and could include a further strengthening of Community structural and regional policies. With the locking of exchange rates the ESCB would assume full responsibility for the conduct of monetary policy and would prepare the transition to a single currency.

Although some aspects of the Delors Committee's proposals for transition to EMU have been disputed, the definitions of stages one, two and three set out above are a guide with which to follow the debate and a yardstick against which to measure the proposals in the new Treaty.

Why the Transition to EMU is Contentious

In considering the question of transition to EMU it is important to recognise that several different issues are involved. Indeed, as will be seen below, member states' approaches to the transition issue reflect a complex combination of economic and political considerations.

First, we can identify an analytical reason why the final shape of EMU and the transition to EMU should be considered together. It is widely recognised that both the nature and the timing of the costs and benefits of EMU are likely to be distributed unevenly. NESC drew attention to this in their analysis of EMU, pointing out that the adjustment costs to monetary or currency integration are *private*, borne by specific individuals and groups, and are incurred *immediately*. By contrast, the benefits of monetary integration are spread very widely and, furthermore, may materialise only in the long run (NESC, 1989, p. 427). For example, adherence to a harder currency link is likely to impose immediate costs on particular individuals and groups in particular countries — specifically those in high-inflation and low-productivity countries whose business and employment is dependent on international cost competitiveness. Conversely, the benefits of monetary integration consist in the convenience of using a uniform money in gathering information and undertaking transactions, and in the predictable, and probably low, inflation which would prevail. All these benefits are spread widely and almost certainly take some time to materialise. Consequently, it is appropriate that issues concerning the transition to monetary union are taken into account in the deciding for or against EMU and in designing the Treaty basis of the system.

But this analysis of the nature and timing of the costs and benefits of EMU should also alert us to the fact that arguments about the desirable transition to EMU should not be taken at face value. While arguments about the transition to EMU are piously couched in technical terms, such as the need for prior nominal convergence, they may also have distributional implications and motivations. Put bluntly, member states may favour a particular speed and pattern of transition, not because it is technically necessary, but because it allows them capture the benefits of EMU while passing the costs elsewhere.

The second reason why the issue of transition to EMU is very significant in the design of EMU is that there are genuine differences of opinion on what amount and kind of convergence is necessary before exchange rates can be permanently locked or abolished, and what action is necessary to achieve that degree of convergence. The answer to this question will influence decisions on the timing of stages two and three.

This issue of how to achieve the requisite convergence should be distinguished from a third, subtly different, one. This concerns the role of the transition as a phase in which the Community learns to coordinate economic policy. An emphasis on this aspect of the transition can be seen in the recent attitude of some member states and the Commission. The background to this emphasis lies in the tension between two somewhat different approaches to European integration — and the current dominance of one of these. One approach is to design the system of political and economic management in advance by reference to a clear analytical model. Others reject what they see as excessive 'system building' and prefer a pragmatic approach in which each element of the regime is created as and when there is intergovernmental agreement on the need for it. Regardless of the general merits of these two approaches, it is arguable that monetary union is special since, unlike most political measures, it cannot be decided on and implemented gradually. However, after a period of dynamic integration, a piecemeal approach seems to have prevailed at both the EMU and political union conferences of 1991. It is this dominance, and the modest constitutional change which follows from it, which leads those who strongly favour EMU to place their faith in the transition as a period in which the Community might *learn* how to run the national economies in a coordinated way. While this may work, and some process of learning was inevitable, it will be important to ask whether the new Treaty is so open as to allow recalcitrant governments to delay the emergence of a common economic policy indefinitely.

The fourth reason for the significance of the transition issue in the design of EMU is that disputes about the transition may, in fact, be disputes about the final shape of EMU and, indeed, of the Community itself. For example, as will be seen below, divergent German and French attitudes to central bank independence have taken the form of different ideas about the content of stage two. Likewise, British opposition to EMU seems, in the context of formal negotiations, to take the form of argument for a long and minimal stage two, with no set date for transition to the final stage. Other member states, particularly Germany, adopt positions on the transition which seem motivated as much by political as economic considerations. While this is perfectly appropriate, it reinforces the point that no argument about the technical economic requirements of transition should be taken at face value.

Each of these five dimensions — the distribution of costs and benefits, convergence requirements, learning to coordinate economic policy, the final shape of EMU and the political — can be seen in the concrete questions concerning transition debated at the 1991 IGC, a few of which we now identify.

The Timing of Stages Two and Three

Much of the current debate on the timing of movement to monetary union reflects a long standing debate within the Community between two groups known as the 'economists' and the 'monetarists' respectively. The economists tend to give priority to the prior harmonisation of economic policies and conditions, while the monetarists believe that monetary integration induces governments to harmonise their economic policies. While it would be mistaken nowadays to counterpose these two views very starkly, there remains significant differences of emphasis. On the one hand, the Commission has recently argued for an early move to monetary union on the grounds, that the danger of severe deflation and unemployment, in high-inflation countries, is less than the traditional 'economist' outlook would suggest and, furthermore that the effects of a hard currency peg in inducing adjustment in both policy and the economy are even greater than the 'monetarists' believed. These two arguments reflect the dominant trend in macroeconomics since the last major debate on EMU in the Community. On the other hand, the evident caution of the richer member states about an early move to an EMU containing all, or most, Community countries suggests that they do not trust in these arguments. In this case a long transition period, or a two-speed EMU, would be desirable (from their point of view) since it would allow the poorer member states to absorb the costs of monetary union before they became members of a full economic and monetary union, and it would minimise the risk of disruption of the existing low-inflation regime. In this, as in the British preference for a long stage two, we can see most of the dimensions of the transition issue listed above.

The Content of Stage Two

A related, but nevertheless separate, issue concerns not the timing but the content of the transitional stage. It was noted above that the Delors Committee advocated a transitional stage in which:

> the basic organs and structure of the economic and monetary union would be set up, involving both the revision of the existing institutions and the establishment of new ones. The institutional framework would gradually take over operational functions, serve as the centre for monitoring and analysing macroeconomic developments and promote a process of common decision-making, with certain operational decisions taken by majority vote. Stage two must be seen as a period of transition to the final stage and would thus primarily constitute a training process leading to collective decision-making, while the ultimate responsibility for policy decisions would remain at this stage with national authorities. The precise operating procedures to be applied in stage two would be developed in the light of prevailing economic conditions and the experience gained in the previous stage (paragraph 55).

This view of the transition attracted opposition on both the monetary and economic fronts. The German government is unwilling to see the new European Central Bank set up before it has the power to run monetary policy. As noted at the start of this section, one suspects that this concern is not only to do with the credibility of the new bank, but reflects an anxiety that other member states, especially the French, would use this transition period to influence the final shape of the EMU. The Delors Committee's vision of a revised institutional framework serving as 'the centre for monitoring and analysing macroeconomic developments' and to 'promote a process of common decision making' has also met considerable opposition.

One Speed or Two Speed

Another actively debated issue concerning the transition to EMU is the question of whether all countries should join EMU together or whether a two-speed system should be envisaged. This issue is, of course, linked to the timing of stages two and three — since it is unlikely that all twelve member states would be in a position to join EMU in the near future. Once again the five dimensions of the transition issue identified above are all relevant. Some member states could achieve the benefits of EMU, while shouldering few of the costs, in a two-speed process. The question of convergence requirements, and the debate between 'economists' and 'monetarists', is clearly relevant. A two-speed union might reduce the difficulty of economic policy coordination and allow those with fundamental hostility to such coordination to opt out. The final shape of the EMU may be less contentious among a subset of member states. Finally, the debate on a one-speed or two-speed EMU clearly reflects significant political differences concerning the nature of the Community. This is most clearly so in the British case, but the shifting position of other governments on this issue also reflects political and, possibly, financial calculations about both national and Europe-wide questions.

Cohesion and the Transition Question

The speed and pattern of transition to EMU has potentially important implications for regional and social disparities in the Community. Consequently, the issue of transition and the cohesion question are related. This aspect of the transition issue is considered when I discuss the implications and issues for Ireland, in the final section of this paper.

The Transition as Defined in the Draft Treaty

The main elements of the transition to EMU envisaged in the new Treaty drafted by the Luxembourg Presidency can be summarised as follows:

Stage I: 1991–1993

Member states take action to:

- free capital movements
- eliminate monetary financing
- adopt multiannual programmes to reduce inflation and budget deficits.

January 1993: establish Board of Governors of central banks

- to replace existing Committee
- run EMS
- strengthen cooperation between central banks
- formulate opinions on monetary policy.

Before end 1993

- Council assess progress on convergence and take necessary action with economic policy instruments.

Stage II (Transitional Stage): January 1994–

January 1994: establish ESCB

January 1996: ESCB begins to operate

ESCB shall:

- promote ecu

– prepare for single monetary policy

– interconnect payments networks

– harmonise monetary statistics

December 1996: Commission and ESCB report to Council on progress towards convergence

Sometime: On basis of report from Council, the European Council sets date for move to Stage III.

It is not easy to interpret these transition provisions. The idea of *establishing* the ESCB at the start of stage two, January, 1994, but having it *come into operation* only in December, 1996 is clearly a compromise between two conflicting views discussed above. However, other aspects of the transition remain unclear. In particular, it is not clear how long stage two will be. Some would interpret the above provisions as a substantial success for those governments that wish to postpone EMU as long as possible. Others can envisage these provisions facilitating movement to EMU well before the end of the century.

In addition, the meaning of these transitions will be substantially conditioned by decisions concerning one- or two-speed EMU. Since it is unlikely that all twelve member states will be in a position to join EMU in the foreseeable future, some kind of phased or two-speed EMU is probably inevitable. The question is, what constitutional and legal formula should be adopted. One option, embodied in the Draft Treaty, is that all member states should participate in principle but that the Council grants temporary derogations during stage two and at the start of stage three. An alternative, which has been canvassed by some governments, is that a subset of the twelve governments should decide to proceed to EMU on their own, setting conditions for entry agreed among themselves. While this might facilitate an earlier move to EMU it could serve to sever EMU from the wider range of Community objectives and policies. These observations serve to illustrate that the transition issue interacts in a complex way with all the other issues in the design of the Community's constitution.

4. IMPLICATIONS AND ISSUES FOR IRELAND

(i) The Main Issues in Brief

This overview of EMU has identified a long list of issues concerning its structure, management and Treaty status. This final section provides some assessment of the relative significance of these issues from an Irish perspective. My argument will be that Ireland has a significant positive interest in parallelism, in economic policy, and in the institutional balance; and a somewhat negative interest in subsidiarity. Finally, the issue of transition to EMU is of potential significance for Ireland.

(ii) A Strategic Approach to European Integration

However, more important than ranking the issues in order of importance is the need to recall some general principles which apply precisely to the present situation. The essence of these principles is that all of the issues which are of any importance must be considered together.

NESC has strongly advocated a strategic approach to European integration, within which, policy on specific matters would be fitted and tactical approaches devised. In explaining the advantages of this approach NESC made a number of points which are relevant in the current situation.

The Package of Treaty Revisions

NESC pointed out that as a result of the collegiate nature of commitments in the Community, agreements frequently consist of *packages* (NESC, 1989, p. 431). In this sense it is important to consider EMU and political union together. One can view the basic package which emerges from the negotiations as having four components: money, security, institutional reforms and, possibly, cohesion. Since each government has particular interests under one or more of these headings no government can avoid a trade-off between them.

The implications of the final package for employment, unemployment and living standards in Ireland are most important from an economic perspective. The key question then is whether the Irish government's approach under the security and institutional reform headings (and also in the parallel negotiations on the CAP), is such as to maximise the achievement on the monetary and cohesion fronts. A subsidiary question is whether the approach to the monetary and cohesion issues are complementary to one another.

The analysis in this paper strongly suggests that these questions are pertinent. Three different kinds of argument each led to the conclusion that the place of the cohesion issue, and power of cohesion-promoting policies, is dependent on the overall scope and content of Community policies, and that these are critically dependent on the degree of 'political homogeneity' or political cohesion.

Overconcentration on Any One Objective

A strategic view in favour of advanced European economic and monetary union may make it easier for Ireland to achieve the objective of real convergence in living standards, employment and unemployment. One reason cited by NESC was that "such an approach allows this objective to be made consistent with the objective of other member states and with the goals of the Community". In this context, NESC made an observation which may be usefully recalled in approaching the issues of monetary union, political union and agricultural reform:

> To establish a given objective as an actual Community priority, it must be consistent with the resolution of the major problems facing the Community in general. There is clear evidence that concentration of any one member state on any one objective is liable to jeopardise the achievement of even that one objective, and certainly undermine the ability of the Community as a whole to address its problems.

(iii) The Priorities Explained

Parallelism

It seems clear that Ireland has a definite interest in the parallel development of 'Community' approaches on the monetary and economic fronts. However, the adoption of this principle by the European Council, at Madrid in June 1989, may not prevent the emergence of a somewhat unbalanced structure — with more coherent institutions and policy on the monetary side than on the economic side. Therefore, Ireland's interests go beyond the (somewhat empty) principle of parallelism to the details of economic policy.

Economic Policy

The aims and execution of economic policy in EMU are of great significance to Ireland. First, as a small, open, economy with little ability to conduct demand management. Ireland has an interest in successful Community coordination of macroeconomic policy. Second, the scope and content of Community microeconomic policies is of considerable interest to Ireland. Third, the counter argument does not apply: Ireland has little reason to resist Community control on national fiscal policies.

Institutional Balance

The Irish people have a distinct interest in the institutional issue for two reasons. First, the achievement of a common economic policy — to balance against the single monetary policy — requires the development of a political body with the authority, capacity and legitimacy to determine an economic policy for the Community. Second, significant advance in the position of the cohesion issue in the Community system — and the enhancement of cohesion policies — requires a change in the relationship between Community institutions and the member states.

These are the reasons why, and the sense in which, the issue of institutional balance is of importance to the Irish people. But it should be clear that they do not determine what precise institutional balance — between the Commission, the Council and the Parliament — would yield these results. Opinions will differ on how the capacity and legitimacy of the main decision-making body, the Council, can be enhanced (see Brigid Laffan's 'The Governance of the Union' and Edward Moxon-Browne's 'The Legitimacy of the Union' in the series *Studies in European Union: Political Union,* IEA, 1991).

Subsidiarity

Although the Irish government has agreed that the principle of subsidiarity is one of the guiding principles in building EMU, it is clear that Ireland's interests would not be served by a strong Treaty provision and a restrictive interpretation of the principle. This is because such an interpretation would serve to limit the scope and content of Community policy, whereas Ireland's interest lies in the appropriate extension of each.

Transition

The issue of transition to EMU is of considerable interest to Ireland. However, it is not easy to say that Ireland has a definite interest in a particular speed of transition. This reflects the complexity of the transition issue and the fact that all the main issues in the design of EMU have a bearing on the transition question.

One of the standard arguments against the rapid movement of poorer countries into a monetary union is that this would involve a sudden severe deflation of the economy with consequent loss of output and employment, and perhaps a permanent loss of manufacturing capacity. It is clear that this argument does not apply in the Irish case, since sufficient disinflation has already been achieved. This suggests that one of the general arguments in favour of rapid movement to EMU applies. It was noted in Section 3 (v) that the benefits of EMU take some time to materialise; this means that an early move to full EMU would bring Ireland into the beneficial phase sooner than a long drawn out transition would. Indeed, the EMS membership can be seen as part of a long, and difficult, transition to EMU. The continuing, and in some respects increasing, difficulty of this half-way-house was noted by NESC in *Ireland in the European Community* (1989, see also O'Donnell, 1991). NESC returned to this subject in its recent report *A Strategy for the Nineties: Economic Stability and Structural Change,* where it analysed Ireland's situation between now and full monetary union in a chapter entitled 'Macroeconomic Policy Without Exchange Controls' (NESC, 1990, Chapter 5). This revealed that because of the structural characteristics of the Irish economy, macroeconomic, and especially monetary, management could be difficult in 'the new EMS' — i.e. the EMS without exchange controls. There is also a political dimension to this argument for an early move to full EMU. Because the costs and benefits of EMU will be distributed unevenly, both between countries and across time, a fairly rapid movement to European monetary union would tend to highlight the links between costs and benefits and thereby place these firmly on the political agenda at Community level. A very slow transition, or a certain kind of two-speed process, would tend to produce less sharing of the costs and benefits.

Although these considerations suggest that Ireland should favour a fast transition to full EMU, there are arguments against this. It was in Section 3 (v) that the current political conjuncture is not favourable to the advance of the cohesion issue within the politics of the Community. In fending off the cohesion issue in the context of the IGCs some member states, and indeed the Commission, have argued that it is too early to judge the regional impact of the completion of the single market, and of the integration process in general. In this context it could be argued that a somewhat longer transition to EMU would allow time for the cohesion case to be developed and advanced within the Community *before* the final system of economic and monetary management is in place. Recall, from Section 3 (iv), that the Delors Report envisaged reviews of the regional question and, if necessary, the enhancement of Community policies, during stages one, two and three of the transition to EMU. In addition, a longer transition may avoid a two-speed EMU and, ultimately, a two-speed Community. There is little doubt that a two-speed Europe is not in Ireland's interest (see NESC, 1989, Chapter 13). However, if these arguments suggest a longer transition period, there is one final complication which should be noted. If it were the case that the formula embodied in the Draft Treaty is the lowest common denominator of what the twelve governments will accept, to such an extent that EMU *may not be achieved at all in the foreseeable future,* then it might be in Ireland's interest to support an early and fast transition — simply to achieve monetary union.

(iv) Looking to the Future

The 1991 Treaty revision is likely to produce a modest deepening of political integration. This means that, in the economic sphere, it will not legislate for, and may not even facilitate, the creation of a political body with the authority, capacity and legitimacy to determine a set of economic policies for the Community. The limited progress on the political front has two important implications for Ireland. First, it may limit the amount of progress that can be made on the cohesion issue in the current revision of the Treaty. However, it strongly suggests that a further Treaty revision could occur later in the decade and, in all probability, before the Community actually moves to a single currency.

This, in turn has two implications for Irish policy, both of which were highlighted by NESC in its report *Ireland in the European Community.* First, membership of the Community does not reduce the need for clear Irish policy aims and methods. NESC emphasised that this applied even where solutions to a problem requires some Community policies and action. Indeed, a study of the factors governing the pattern of production across countries confirms that indigenous factors — including social and political structures and economic policies — can have a significant effect. This suggests that as well as addressing the problem of cohesion at national level, to the extent that this can be done, Ireland must make a leading contribution to the analysis of regional problems and the formulation of Community cohesion policies. But, to date, Irish policy makers, economists, employers organisations and trade unions cannot claim to be leaders in either of these fields.

The second implication of the fact that another Treaty revision is likely in a few years time is that it affords the opportunity to advance the place of the cohesion issue in the Community system. This requires that the analysis of regional problems, referred to above, will have clarified the possible routes to greater cohesion and, indeed, the meaning of cohesion and peripherality. Where this indicates the need for Community policies, thought must be given to how this is to be achieved. In this very context, NESC made the point that "the process of determining Community priorities occurs not only in the European Council, but also in the Commission, the Parliament and, most importantly, *in the society at large*". NESC cited the example of the priority given to the single market in recent years; the urgency of this was established in the society and it became an imperative which government ministers throughout the Community could not ignore. This implies that if the objective of regional and social cohesion is to be established as a higher Community priority between now and the next Treaty revision it "must be advocated by arguments of the highest quality in the widest possible forum. Ireland, both its Government and its people, must play a leading role on this debate" (NESC, 1989).

Two years later, with a further revision of the Treaty in process, that argument has even greater force. The movement from the Single Act and the single market programme to the design of an economic and monetary union, has been more rapid than many thought possible. The speed of this movement, and yet the limits of the current Treaty revision, has highlighted the importance of the political element and the link between economic and political integration. Thought must be given to the nature of this link and to the best strategy for harnessing its potential and transcending its current limits.

BIBLIOGRAPHY

Delors, J. (1989), *Report on Economic and Monetary Union in the European Community*. Luxembourg: Office for Official Publications of the European Communities.

Goodhart, C. (1989), *Money, Information and Uncertainty*. Second edition. London: Macmillan.

Harden, I. (1990), 'EuroFed or Monster Bank', *National Westminster Bank Quarterly Review*, August.

Laffan, B. (1984), 'The Politics of Redistribution in the European Community', *Administration*, Vol. 32, No. 2.

Molle, W. (1990), *The Economics of European Integration: Theory, Practice, Policy*. Dartmouth: Aldershot.

MacDougall, D. (1977), *Report of the Study Group on the Role of Public Finance in European Integration*, Vols. 1 and 2 (The MacDougall Report). Brussels: European Commission.

NESC (1989), *Ireland in the European Community: Performance, Prospects and Strategy*. Dublin: National Economic and Social Council.

NESC (1990), *A Strategy for the Nineties: Economic Stability and Structural Change*. Dublin: National Economic and Social Council.

O'Donnell, R. (1991), 'Monetary Policy', *Ireland and EC Membership Evaluated*, ed. P. Keatinge. London: Pinter.

Padoa-Schioppa, F. (1987), *Efficiency, Stability and Equity: A Strategy for the Evolution of the Economies of the Economic System of the European Community*. Oxford: Oxford University Press.

Pelkmans, J. (1982), 'The Assignment of Public Functions in Economic Integration', *Journal of Common Market Studies*, Vol. 21, Nos. 1 and 2, September/December.

Pelkmans, J. and Robson, P. (1987), 'The Aspirations of the White Paper', *Journal of Common Market Studies*, Vol. 25, No. 3.

Pinder, J. (1968), 'Positive and Negative Integration: Some Problems of Economic Union in the EEC'.

Pinder, J. (1987), 'Is the Single European Act a Step Towards a Federal Europe?', *Policy Studies*, Vol. 7, Part 4, April.

Robson, P. (1987), *The Economics of International Integration*. London: Allen and Unwin, third edition.

Swann, P. (1987), *The Economcis of the European Community*. Harmondsworth: Penguin.

Werner, P. (1970), *Economic and Monetary Union in the Community*. Luxembourg: Office for Official Publications of the European Communities.

MONETARY UNION

Patrick Honohan

EXECUTIVE SUMMARY

Since the publication of the Delors Report on Economic and Monetary Union (EMU), political and technical discussion has focused on making operational a package of policy initiatives taking integration in the Community beyond the point it will have reached with the completion of the single market. As it is emerging in negotiations, this next stage will primarily involve the establishment of a monetary union with a single currency. There will be other measures, including some procedures to limit national budget deficits and perhaps some increase in international transfers to help lagging regions. The focus in this paper is on the monetary union; the fiscal aspects are only treated incidentally.

The motivation for a monetary union is a double one: on the one hand, the convenience and certainty of having just one currency in the single market is more or less obvious; on the other hand, the difficulty of shaking off the inflationary experience of the past two decades has led several Community countries to seek the stability which could be provided by adopting a currency managed by a strong, independent and supranational central bank.

The ability of activist monetary policy to influence output and employment is less now than it was thought to be in the past. Therefore, although price stability will be the central objective of the monetary union, that need not imply that employment will be sacrificed. Indeed, a stable macroeconomic environment should be conducive to investment and growth supportive of employment.

As it is evolving in the debate, the institutional framework for the proposed European Central Bank (ECB) is based substantially on that of the German Bundesbank. The negotiators clearly accept the need for an ECB that is independent of government in the sense that its Council need take instructions from neither national nor community governmental institutions. But one wonders whether it is wise to retain the national central banks (however limited their expected role in EMU). By ensuring that the governors of the national central banks form a majority on the ECB Council, the designer of the new institution may unwittingly be storing up problems of excessive regional autonomy. Furthermore, it is arguable that the ultimate responsibility for prudential supervision of banks (as well as that for monetary policy) should be transferred to the ECB. Experience in the Third World with regionally decentralised central banks is extremely discouraging.

Increased competition facing Irish banks and the rest of the financial sector in the years ahead probably derives more from the completion of the single market and from the elimination of exchange controls than from the single currency *per se*, and it could be especially acute during the transition. The Irish banking system, like that in other small countries, will have its work cut out to remain competitive in the new regime. They will need to take action to reduce their costs. Government should also ensure (without giving them special protection) that local banks are not disadvantaged relative to banks from partner countries. A loss of market share by Irish banks could lead to their having a reduced capacity to lend, possibly creating difficulties, at least in the short-run, for small Irish borrowers whose creditworthiness is known only to local bankers.

Currency risk as a source of nominal interest rate differentials in the Community will be eliminated by the common currency, just as the removal of exchange controls under the 1992 Programme has already helped the convergence of real interest rates. Ireland in the EMU would have lower nominal and real wholesale interest rates than an Ireland that stayed outside. The present exchange rate regime almost guarantees higher interest rates in Ireland than could be achieved under EMU. For this reason we have argued that it is in Ireland's interest that the transition to the single currency should be brief.

1. INTRODUCTION

Since the publication of the Delors Report on Economic and Monetary Union, political and technical discussion has focused on making operational a package of policy initiatives taking integration in the Community beyond the point it will have reached with the completion of the single market. As it is emerging in negotiations, the economic aspects of this next stage known as EMU, will primarily involve the establishment of a monetary union with a single currency. There will be other measures, including some procedures to limit national budget deficits and perhaps some increase in international transfers to help lagging regions. As to whether establishment of a monetary union in Europe actually requires ancillary action in order to be worthwhile, there is undoubtedly scope for different opinions. It would surely be all the better if there were further explicit accompanying fiscal measures built in, but a workable monetary union can arguably be successful even without such measures. Whatever about that, the central initiative in the EMU will be the monetary union, and that is the focus of this paper.

The paper is organised as follows. The next section discusses the motivation for a monetary union drawing on the recent literature which emphasises the desirability of a strong independent central bank in Europe with the credibility that is needed to preserve price stability without damaging employment. Section 3 evaluates the institutional framework for the EMU as it is evolving in the debate, addressing in particular the membership of the Council of the European Central Bank, and the degree to which national central banks should continue to have policy functions, including the prudential supervision of banks. Section 4 considers the limitations of monetary union: how serious the loss of monetary independence might be in the new system when it is in operation; and the specific difficulties which may be faced by the banking systems of small countries. The timeframe and mechanics of transition are analysed in Section 5 which argues against undue delay in proceeding to full monetary union. Finally, Section 6 contains some concluding remarks.

2. THE OBJECTIVES OF A MONETARY UNION

(i) Monetary Union: Convenience and Stability

Those who have been pushing for a monetary union in Europe have had two principal objectives which are not at first sight closely related. The first can be termed convenience, the second stability.

The idea of a single market throughout Europe with the minimum of frontiers, physical or otherwise, leads naturally to the proposal that there should only be one currency. The single currency would eliminate currency conversion costs as well as uncertainty about the future relative values of different currencies. In Ireland, we were used to the convenience of having no currency conversion costs and effectively no uncertainty about exchange risks for about one half or more of our foreign trade in the decades before the Sterling link was broken.[1]

The stability argument starts from a completely different concern. Observers note that inflation in Germany over the past two decades has been far lower than that experienced in several surges by other European countries, not least Ireland, but also Britain, Denmark and the Mediterranean countries. The underlying reasons for the differing experiences have been extensively discussed. The various inflationary shocks that have hit European countries have not been so diverse as to allow an external explanation for the different inflation rates. The response of monetary and fiscal policy to these shocks has however been different, and there have been home-grown inflations too where the initial impulse came from within each economy. Anti-inflationary policy has failed to be fully credible in these countries (as witness conspicuously the resurgence of inflation in the UK during 1989–90 after the costly disinflation of the previous decade). Those who seek stability wish to tie policy to that of the German monetary and fiscal authorities in order to benefit from the credibility which they have established and which has given Germany low inflation for so long.

The attempt to achieve stability by linking to the DM was initiated by France in 1978 with proposals for the establishment of the European Monetary System (EMS), which began operating in March 1979. Ireland and Italy also joined the EMS at the time, though it seems fair to say that their decision to join was driven as much by a desire to remain in the forefront of moves towards greater integration in Europe as a desire to achieve monetary stability.[2] In the event (and contrary to the expectations of all involved), the EMS proved to be a softer currency regime for Ireland than the Sterling link would have been, as the start

---

[1]Estimates of the direct and indirect costs involved in currency fluctuations are generally in the range of 0.2 to 0.4 per cent of GDP, say £50–£100 million per annum in Ireland.

[2]The wide six per cent margins chosen by Italy meant that it experienced little discipline from the exchange rate mechanism, especially considering the frequent devaluations of the lira in the early years of the system. Both Ireland and Italy received subsidies from the remainder of the Community to help compensate for the costs of transition to a hard currency regime.

of the EMS more or less coincided with the start of a period of extremely tight monetary policy in Britain.[3] Only on one day since the link was broken has the Irish pound ever touched parity with sterling.

The first eight years of the EMS produced only mixed evidence in favour of the idea that a currency arrangement of that type could deliver stability. Admittedly, inflation rates had fallen across the board: but so had inflation rates in non-EMS countries. And the frequent realignments — more than one a year — meant that the DM had appreciated by as much as 46 per cent against the Irish pound, 49 per cent against the French franc and 73 per cent against the Italian lira. It seemed that a tighter currency link would be required to achieve the sought-after stability.

Since 1987, conditions have been more favourable for currency stability in Europe. The lower inflation rates that have been achieved have meant that pressures for realignment on competitiveness grounds have been less severe than before, and this has helped financial markets to take more seriously official statements that realignments are a thing of the past. Nevertheless, it is quite possible that the past four years may prove to have been exceptionally stable. Full adherence of the pound sterling to the system may yet prove to be a destabilising factor in itself. Not until the possibility of realignment is eliminated will exchange rate stability within Europe and the corresponding price level stability have been fully secured.

A new consideration favouring the establishment of a monetary union has arisen since the unification of Germany has placed a question mark against the previously impeccable stability provided by the German authorities. It now becomes necessary to consider whether Germany is able, on its own, to carry the burden of stability for the Community: perhaps for this reason alone a new and independent monetary institution in Europe would be required.

Stability and convenience might appear to be wholly unrelated objectives: the one macroeconomic, the other microeconomic, but on consideration they are not wholly divorced from one another. After all, the convenience of having a single currency would be negated if its own value, in terms of goods and non-European currencies, were unstable. This then is a link between the two objectives driving the move towards monetary union in Europe.

(ii) Securing Credibility

If achieving credibility by tying one's currency to the policies of a strong, independent central bank is an important objective of the exercise, one would

[3]Not until October 1990 did the UK become a participant in the exchange rate mechanism of the EMS; accordingly the sterling link was broken just two weeks after the start of EMS when its maintenance became incompatible with the agreed margins of fluctuation for the Irish pound.

like to be sure that the particular way in which this is being approached does achieve the desired result. For it is not the case that each of the member states is actually relinquishing its currency and adopting the Deutsche mark. Instead, a new currency and a new institutional structure is to be set up. Can one ensure that this new structure and currency will not represent a least common denominator among the members in terms of anti-inflation policy? Does it require that the process of inflation should be divorced from other economic policy and given to a distinct agency dedicated to achieving price stability alone? Or conversely, must one recognise that a blinkered anti-inflation bias could plunge the whole of Europe into a recession and, if so, must monetary policy (and exchange rate policy for the common currency) be seen as an integral component of overall economic policy and adapted to the evolving macroeconomic situation? These questions go to the heart of the debate on the limitations of monetary policy and how it can best be exercised.

There is, as yet, no supranational European government. Nor do the discussions on Political Union and EMU envisage a single fiscal authority with anything like the dominance of central governments even in federal states. For this reason, to assign the management of a common currency to a EC-level institution has some of the characteristics of a partial privatisation: the area of currency and monetary policy is being moved further from direct government influence.

Legal and institutional arrangements governing the degree of government control over monetary matters at present differ widely in the Community. A legacy of the Sterling link in Ireland has been considerable statutory autonomy for the central bank. During the Sterling link period, the scope for activist monetary policy was extremely limited, and was left to the central bank probably because it was seen as being a largely technical matter. Nevertheless, monetary policy in Ireland is not carried out without an awareness of government policy. And in other countries governments have even more of a say in the formulation of monetary policy. The Bank of England, for example, enjoys much less statutory autonomy than the Central Bank of Ireland. Thus, each member state, by transferring authority for currency and monetary matters to a common authority, would be removing an important source of government control in this area. Insofar as all countries would be pooling their resources in this area, no single government would retain traditional powers.

The notion of, to put it provocatively, relinquishing the management of monetary matters to a quasi-non-governmental agency is supported by economic theorists who have noted that political pressures may make it all but impossible for a government to achieve the balance of low inflation and high levels of output which all desire. According to what is now a widely-accepted — if somewhat paradoxical — theory, it seems likely that, by abjuring the right to influence monetary policy the government can in fact achieve a better balance of inflation and employment.[4] This is what has been termed "the advantage of tying one's hands behind one's back" (Giavazzi and Pagano, 1988).

One could consider seeking price stability by abandoning fiduciary paper currency altogether and using a commodity standard (like gold). This could be done as in the past by requiring one hundred per cent gold backing for any paper currency that was issued; bank reserves would likewise have to be held in the form of gold or gold-backed assets. A gold anchor should normally have the effect that inflation does not get out of hand (16th century Spain being an exception), and indeed the latter part of the 19th century was marked by falling prices in countries attached to the gold standard. However attractive the idea of a pure commodity standard may seem from an anti-inflation point of view, experience shows that it would not be sufficiently flexible to cope with panics and other surges of market sentiment. The lack of an elastic supply of liquidity has converted many a panic into a recession, notably in the 19th century. Accordingly, it is generally felt that a central bank, with the power to create liquidity as needed, is essential to the smooth operation of modern economies (and indeed the Bank of England deviated several times from the strict application of Gold Standard rules during the 19th century in order to head off a panic). It is for this reason that little opposition is heard to the idea that the EMU should have, at its centre, an European Central Bank (ECB).

In arranging that monetary policy is franchised to the ECB on a long-term basis, it is clear that price stability will be at the centre of the objectives to be pursued by the ECB. Indeed the theoreticians point out that a consequence of this way of thinking about monetary policy is that it could be preferable for the governing authority of the Bank to attach a greater weight to price stability than does the government itself (Rogoff, 1985). There are clearly risks here: undue conservatism (especially in the face of inflationary shocks) could lead to severe policy errors. The British return to gold and US monetary policy at the outset of the great depression of the 1930s are the usual examples provided. However, the establishment of an independent central bank removes an actual inflationary bias. By choosing the central bank's governing council well, the EC governments should be able to avoid a systematic bias in the opposite direction.

The way in which the ECB will pursue price stability — following current central bank practice — is to influence the price and quantity of bank liquidity to

[4]The argument runs something like the following: For many governments, a modest monetary expansion will often seem attractive if it can achieve high output and employment without triggering excessive inflation. But unions and firms in setting wage and price contracts will build in to their inflation expectations, and thus into their wage claims and pricing strategy, this known preference of governments. The result is inevitably more inflation with no gain in output. If governments were able to pre-commit themselves to avoiding opportunist monetary expansion, then the problem would not arise (Kydland and Prescott, 1977).

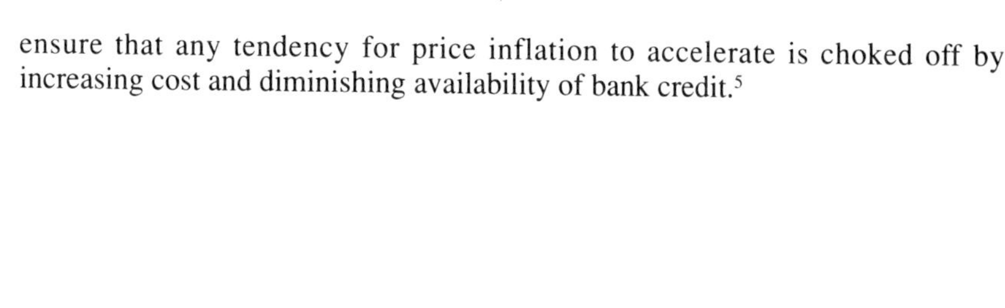

ensure that any tendency for price inflation to accelerate is choked off by increasing cost and diminishing availability of bank credit.[5]

[5]Many economists speak of 'base money' rather than bank liquidity as being the appropriate focus of central banking policy. But base money is just the sum of currency in circulation outside banks and the reserves of the banks. The real aim (since currency is supplied freely on demand) is to influence the interest rates on the volume of bank reserves or bank liquidity. This is the fulcrum on which monetary policy is levered. The cheaper and more readily accessible are bank reserves, the readier the banks will be to extend credit. The more plentiful credit and money, the greater the spending power driving up prices and also leading to external deficits.

3. THE INSTITUTIONAL STRUCTURE

(i) A System of Central Banks or a Single Central Bank?

A recurrent ambiguity in recent discussions on the EMU is whether the new institutional arrangements for monetary policy will be a coordinated system of national central banks or a single central bank for the whole of the Community with essentially dependent national agencies. Draft Treaty revisions currently being circulated envisage a "European System of Central Banks, comprising the European Central Bank and the national central banks". Since the whole EMU debate is about the degree to which monetary matters should be on a common basis throughout the Community, it is not surprising that this question of the degree of centralisation is crucial.

The tension between these two views has actually been a feature of policy debate in relation to most large federal economies and in relation to the other currency unions in the world today. Arguably, this is one of the most important institutional issues to be resolved, and like many other issues, it will not, in practice, be fully resolved until the new arrangements have evolved through periods of pressure or crisis.

This was certainly the experience of the US Federal Reserve System, the apparent legal autonomy of whose twelve regional Reserve Banks has, in practice, proved to be nugatory. For instance, though they disputed this at first, they cannot set independent interest rates for their lending to commercial banks; their dealing in government securities — even more important for influencing liquidity conditions — is wholly determined by the System Open Market Manager in New York. While the regional Reserve Banks are represented on the key Open Market Committee, they are outnumbered by the Governors of the System based in Washington.

Unlike the US case, the executive directors of the German Bundesbank are in a minority on the Bundesbank Central Council. However, in other respects, the federal nature of the Bundesbank is more apparent than real, especially after a 1957 revision of the statutes which clarified the legal dependence of the eleven[6] Ländeszentralbanken on the central bank.[7]

The maintenance of central control in the countries mentioned so far has obviously been made a lot easier by virtue of the strong central government and relatively homogeneous legal system in each country. These conditions will not prevail in Europe, at least for some time (as they have not prevailed in the two examples to which we turn below). Therefore, greater reliance may have to be placed on statutory definition of the powers of national central banks than is the case in relation to regional central banks in the US and Germany.

---

[6]It is anticipated that the number of Ländeszentralbanken will be increased to accommodate the Länder of East Germany.

[7]The Bank of England and the Bank of France are even more centralised, with very little autonomy for the regional branches.

Two examples may be mentioned where insufficient central control has led to serious problems. In China, the provincial branches of the People's Bank (whose managers are appointed by the provincial political authorities) have tended to expand liquidity to support local needs against the wishes of the Head Office of the People's Bank. The resulting surges of inflation in China during the 1980s were stemmed only by draconian action by the highest political authorities in Beijing. The banking problems of the two largest currency unions in the world, those of the French franc zone in Africa,[8] may be attributed in part to a similar lack of central control. Here the problem has not just been one of excessive overall credit expansion, but of imprudent lending by the central bank to poorly-managed commercial banks. This has occurred mostly in the larger countries of each of the unions, and the decisions have effectively been taken by the National Agencies (each of which is headed by a national of the country in which it is located).

A review of regional autonomy in some of the most relevant central banks around the world suggests two conclusions. First, whatever institutional arrangements are made at the outset, the exact balance of powers is likely to remain a contentious issue in the early years of EMU and will certainly evolve over time. Second, national political pressures are likely to be more effective the more power is decentralised in the European system of central banks. Not only will this tend to weaken the anti-inflationary stance of policy overall, which would be in nobody's interest, but the larger and more politically powerful countries are more likely to prevail in a decentralised system. Perhaps it is too soon to speak of the abolition of national central banks, but the ultimate logic of our reasoning seems open to that conclusion.

(ii) The Council: Its Membership and Powers

Discussions so far appear to have reached a considerable degree of consensus on the institutional arrangements for the governing council of the European Central Bank. Following the German model, it is envisaged that the ECB Council will be composed of the President of the ECB, four or five other executive members — the senior management of the ECB — plus the governors of the national central banks. Note immediately that this balance leaves the executive members in a minority on the council. This is a definite contrast with the US model and seems to put in place a structural weakness of the centre *vis-a-vis* the national central banks. One may also be forgiven for wondering how this model can cope with the possible progressive enlargement of the Community. Even with twelve member states, the model creates a very large Council — probably too large for real working sessions. It is not absurd to think of six or eight new member states in the Community over the next twenty years (after all there have been six

[8]The Union Monetaire Ouest Africaine and the Banque des Etats de l'Afrique Centrale cover respectively seven countries in West Africa and six in Central Africa.

newcomers in the last two decades). Will the statutes of the ECB have to be changed fundamentally to deal with this new situation?

Another problem with the proposed arrangement is that it makes no numerical concession to the larger member states. The Council of Ministers does operate in this manner, but in a political arena where the economic strength of each minister clearly plays a role in the final agreements. The European Central Bank will be an independent agency, so the statutory voting powers will be decisive. For how long will, for example, the German authorities remain happy with a situation which gives them only one vote in twenty or more?

The powers of the ECB Council will be far-reaching ones.[9] The ECB Council will have the last word on all aspects of monetary policy — interest rates, liquidity management and, presumably, the external value of the ecu.

This last point must be qualified, for the choice of exchange rate regime, as might arise if there were to be some new worldwide agreement on an exchange rate system, is likely to be reserved to the political level. That the choice of exchange rate regime can be reserved for political decision should not lead to any expectation that week-to-week exchange rate movements could likewise be subject to political influence. After all, decisions on the external value of the ecu can hardly be divorced from policy on liquidity and interest rate conditions within the Union. A tight monetary policy with high interest rates and scarce liquidity will attract capital from abroad. Though restrictions on such capital movements may not be altogether ruled out, the effectiveness of such restrictions would be very limited indeed for the ecu market.

Accordingly, the inflow pressure would tend to put upward pressure on the external value of the ecu, unless the central bank was prepared to buy, e.g. US dollars in order to hold down the ecu. Conversely, a lax monetary policy will tend to put downward pressure on the external value of the ecu. Any attempt to make the external value of the ecu the subject of some separate political control is likely to fall foul of these inter-relationships.

Modern central banks operate in a different manner to those of only a few years ago. Instead of posting fixed official interest rates (such as 'bank rate', the discount rate, or the Lombard rate) at which it is prepared to lend to the commercial banks at their initiative, the typical central bank now becomes involved on its own initiative in influencing liquidity conditions and market interest rates in a very flexible manner. Thus the central bank is typically active on a daily basis in buying and selling short-term securities, either outright or with an agreement to repurchase. Instead of dealing with each commercial bank with a view to meeting the specific liquidity needs of that bank, the central bank deals with the market in general, knowing that its purchase of securities will release

---

[9]Though unlikely to be given any special powers, the President of the Council is likely to be especially influential.

liquidity to the market which in turn will ensure that the liquidity reaches the banks that need it most. This method of operation has several advantages. It allows the central bank to obtain a better feel for overall liquidity conditions than it would otherwise obtain if banks always turned to it for help and the market for short-term funds was therefore inactive. Second, by removing a prop which will be generally relied upon by those banks which are not able to mobilise deposit resources, it helps to ensure that the most efficient banks can grow at the expense of the less efficient. Third, it allows the central bank to influence market interest rates quickly and without formality, in contrast to the heavy statutory procedures which are often involved in changing posted official rates.

This flexibility is obtained at the cost of a considerable increase in operational complexity. The instruments being employed require day-by-day and even hour-by-hour modulation in order to achieve the desired objectives. It remains to be seen in what way the ECB Council will express its policy decisions for implementation and how it will monitor the implementation of those decisions. For the present, it appears to be envisaged that the national central banks will be the implementing agents. As already mentioned, allowing the national central banks any considerable degree of discretion in implementation presents risks.

(iii) Independence of the Central Bank

In line with the objective of distancing governments from the operation of monetary policy, most observers argue that the ECB should be 'independent'. This independence is to be thought of as being *vis-a-vis* both national governments and the Community government in its various components, including the Commission, the Parliament, the Council of Ministers and the European Council. Somewhat tautological evidence has been adduced that more independent central banks have been more successful in limiting inflation. In reality, for countries that have them, the independence of the central bank and the low inflation have both sprung from a deep political consensus that inflation needs to be contained. Nevertheless, it is clear that little will be achieved along the road to gaining credibility for low inflation if the ECB is seen as being an instrument under the control of governments some of whom have a very poor record on inflation. "It is essential to recognise that the ECB's success in achieving low inflation depends on its ability to function in a complex political environment" (National Economic and Social Council – NESC, 1990). A central bank that is not sensitive to political realities will see its power eroded, one way or another.

Having said that, it is worth exploring what is meant by independence and what can reasonably be built into the statutes of the ECB.[10] First, it is desirable

10The classification presented here draws on the April 1991 report of the self-styled 'European System of Central Banks Group'.

that the ECB should have the freedom of action offered by formalised institutional independence, i.e. the legal authority to do what is necessary without constantly requiring government approval. The indications are that this will be written into the Statutes of the central bank and that in addition member states will be called upon to amend domestic legislation as necessary to ensure that the national central banks have the corresponding institutional independence that this entails. Second, there should be material independence, so that the day-to-day workings of the Bank, are not compromised by practical obstruction from government agencies. A legislative protection here is the proposed restriction preventing the ECB from purchasing government securities directly from any national governments; but this is an area where the political skills of the Bank will be more decisive than any statutory powers.[11] Third, there should be personal independence guaranteed through security of tenure and sufficiently long terms of appointment of the executive directors, and the governors of the national central banks. There is general agreement that this too will be provided for. Finally, the Bank should have financial independence guaranteed by an adequate source of revenue.[12]

There is a clear tension between the need for independence and the call for accountability.[13] Parliamentarians in particular often seek to have the central bank held to account for its actions. However, if we accept the view that the business of money management is being abjured by the democratically-elected government ('to save it from itself') we can hardly expect the Parliament to have a role in second-guessing ECB policy. Of course, the Parliament can perform a very useful function in communicating with the management of the ECB, and the reports of the management to the Parliament can provide a useful means of allowing the ECB to make its policies and actions understood in terms of the functions for which it was set up. This is the nature, for example, of the relationship between Congress and the US Federal Reserve Chairman. The skill of the ECB President in dealing with this political environment will be an important factor in determining the degree of political support which is forthcoming for the Bank and its policies.

The NESC report mentioned above argued that the social partners should have a function in the area of monetary policy. NESC recognised that the day-to-day nature of central bank decision-making precluded a close determination by a representative body of the details of monetary policy. It is, however, important

---

[11]It is easy for central banks to support the government's funding programme indirectly without buying government paper directly. By buying private sector securities the central bank frees more private savings for placement in government paper.

[12]The financial position of most central banks has been assured by the structuring of their balance sheet which usually generates a large operating surplus.

[13]A pejorative dichotomy is sometimes drawn between independence and democracy. The difficulty of establishing credibility which we have described reveals this to be a false dichotomy: according to this perspective the will of the people is not served by enabling the government to intervene routinely in monetary policy.

to be clear about the limits in this area. NESC did not specify in any detail what the institutional role of the social partners might be. Though there is no objection in principle against having a minority of non-executive directors drawn from different walks of life, it is doubtful that the ECB Council could or should be representative of the social partners as such. For one thing, this would clearly conflict with what appears to be a fairly firm decision to have the national central bank governors on the ECB Council. But note further that an ECB council formed largely of representation from the social partners is incompatible with the perspective that the decision-making process of the ECB should in some instances lead to policy actions which differ from what would be decided by government on a short-term perspective. Even a consultative role for the social partners would be limited: they could not be given the right to prior consultation on interest rate changes, for example. While the desirability of a good channel of communication should be open between the ECB and legitimate bodies representative of different interests in the Community, the precise institutional mechanism for achieving this is not easy to map at this stage.

One form of political influence that has been proposed over the Bank is that the President of the EcoFin Council should have the right to attend meetings of the ECB Council. (There would be a reciprocal right for the ECB President to attend relevant EcoFin meetings). The idea is a good one in that it provides for good communications between the two bodies. Because the President of EcoFin could hardly be seen as having a weight comparable to that of a Finance minister *vis-a-vis* a national central bank his presence would hardly be an intimidating one sufficient to compromise the ECB's independence. In addition, however, it has been suggested that the EcoFin should have the power to impose a delay on the implementation of any ECB policy. Such a power could only be exercised extremely rarely, and it is hard to see how it could work in practice, with the more flexible operating procedures of modern central banks, and the frequent need for decisive action.

(iv) Prudential Regulation and Supervision of Financial Institutions

Increasing attention has been paid in recent years to the area of prudential regulation of financial institutions. The most conspicuous reason for this has been the well-publicised collapse of an appreciable segment of the housing banks (savings and loan institutions) in the United States at a colossal budgetary cost. Failures of financial institutions are not a new phenomenon in any country, and there have been isolated cases at home (the largest of them in the insurance sector rather than in banking) as well as in the UK, Germany and elsewhere. However, liberalisation of financial markets and an increased volatility of macroeconomic conditions in the last two decades has exposed banks to a greater degree of risk than was the case in the 1950s and 1960s.

The European banking system is often thought of as less vulnerable than that in many other parts of the world partly because of the high degree of concentration in most EC banking systems, with large banks operating on a nationwide basis and thus able to absorb region-specific or sector loan losses. However, it must be recalled that in the early 1980s, the Rumasa crisis in Spain brought failure to some twenty per cent of the domestic banking system. Furthermore, many state-owned Greek and Portuguese banks are thought to be carrying a large burden of doubtful or non-performing loans, mostly to state enterprises. As already mentioned, completion of the single market and progress towards EMU will tend to put pressure on such banks. Even if these banks will surely be rescued by the fiscal or monetary authorities, the instability of these banking systems compromises the efficient functioning of a single European market in banking.

The two keys to a sound banking system are a relatively undistorted incentive framework within which to operate and an effective system of supervision and regulation. On the first, attention must be given to problems of international differentials in financial sector taxation which could weaken the competitive position of banks in some countries *vis-a-vis* those in other countries: a bank whose capital base is weakened by poor profitability is prone to making risky decisions. The availability of deposit insurance can also weaken the system by making substantial deposit funds available to inexperienced or risk-prone bankers. Each EC country now has a formal system of deposit insurance in place. Most are restricted to protecting small depositors and are unlikely to pose as severe problems as did the over-generous scheme in the United States. As deposit insurance is not uniform throughout the Community, there are moves now to harmonise the schemes in the context of the move to EMU. In any such harmonisation, care will have to be taken to ensure that the harmonised system of deposit insurance is not open to abuse.

If capital adequacy requirements are sufficiently strong and there are adequate early warning systems, it should be possible to ensure that bank failures are rare, as indeed they have been in Ireland. Failures actually occur only when the bank has insufficient liquidity to meet requirements, but experience shows that problems with the loan portfolio are generally present long before liquidity becomes an issue. The higher the loan losses, the easier it is for bank inspectors to detect the problem. The higher the equity capital in the bank, the more loan losses can be taken before the deposits are placed at risk. Thus the combination of high capital requirements and thorough inspection is necessary. There is a tendency to feel that the Basle Agreement on a worldwide harmonised capital adequacy standard has resolved the first of these issues. However, though that agreement was a triumph of diplomacy and compromise, the standards actually agreed may not be adequate against the background of increasing awareness of the vulnerability of banks to failure. The ECB could spearhead pressure to increase the levels of capital in a further round of Basle talks so that the widespread problems of US banking, and the potential problems of Japanese banking, do not spill over into Europe.

There has been a discussion of how far banking supervision should remain decentralised in the EMU. The expectation is that, although the ECB will have a role here, it will mainly be a coordinating role. If so, an opportunity may be missed. A significant contribution to the US savings and loan failures was the fact that regionally decentralised supervisory authorities succumbed to local pressures and allowed unsound banks to stay in operation. Exactly the same thing occurred in the franc zone, where the separation of powers between the multinational central bank and the national bank licensing authorities was fatal. The central bank provided liquidity to bolster failing banks while the licensing authority — ignoring early warning signs, and fearful of adverse political reaction to closing banks run by, or for, well-connected persons — failed to act. This pattern is entirely predictable. The first thing that an unscrupulous banker will do to protect himself from the regulator is to generate local dependent interests; the banker typically has the means to do this. Nor is this an overly cynical view: official studies have shown that fraud or insider abuse has been a contributing factor to as many as one in every two US bank failures (US Office of the Comptroller of the Currency, 1988).

US savings and loan supervision has now been centralised under the authority of the federal Treasury Department. Reform in the franc zone (spearheaded by the intervention of the French Treasury) is taking the form of the establishment of an union-wide bank supervision authority. The same approach should be considered for the EMU.

While the 'white paper doctrine' of home country control was the key to achieving completion of the single market, it should probably be seen only as a transitional stage insofar as bank supervision and control is concerned. Arguably, a centralised bank supervision authority (whether a department of the ECB or a separate entity) with wide powers, would be more able to operate above national political pressures in acting decisively to prevent a failing bank from continuing to operate in an unsound manner. There would, of course, be a need to retain a local-based inspection system for supplying the local feel which is essential for detecting the early warning signs of distress. But, so far as action to restrain unsound banking practices is concerned, here again, as in the case of monetary management, it may be worthwhile for national governments to cede power to the centre in order to 'save them from themselves'.

(v) Distribution of Seigniorage

By virtue of the fact that their liabilities comprise non-interest bearing currency notes, as well as bank reserves which often carry interest rates well below market rates, central banks generally make substantial profits from earning interest on their assets — including foreign exchange reserves and a portfolio of government securities. The profits of the central bank can in fact best be thought of as representing the proceeds of a tax on users of currency and on the banking system and its customers. In inflationary times this tax is very high: nominal returns on the central bank's assets soar, whereas currency still pays no interest. Countries with high and unremunerated reserve requirements experience even higher levels of this tax. Most of the profits are usually transferred to the government. This kind of financial sector tax is usually termed seigniorage.[14] Among EC countries, seigniorage has been high in recent decades in Ireland, Italy, Portugal and Spain. As inflation has fallen, this source of government revenue has tended to shrink. It has been calculated that in Portugal these revenues reached as much as seven per cent of GNP in some recent years. Under the EMU a low rate of inflation is anticipated. Likewise, there will be no possibility for highly distorting reserve requirements. Accordingly, the flow of seigniorage will not be very great. In broad terms one can anticipate little more than 0.5 per cent of GNP as the annual flow.

Several authors have expressed concern that the distribution of the EMU seigniorage could be the source of substantial distortions; they have evidently neglected the fact that seigniorage in EMU will be far lower than that experienced in high inflation countries with distorted financial systems. Nevertheless, 0.5 per cent of EC GNP is a significant magnitude (say, 20 billion ecu or about IR£15 billion), and it is certainly worth considering how it should be distributed.

Two main ideas have come to the fore here. One is to have the distribution fixed in accordance with some formula based on the relative size of member states. This would correspond to rules used in African currency unions, which are partly based on local currency circulation. Since the seigniorage tax comes largely from holders of currency, this seems a fair way of making the distribution. However, it is somewhat difficult to determine the national breakdown of currency holdings in a currency union, so inevitably one falls back on some approximate way of gauging currency holdings. The Committee of Governors of EC Central Banks are reported to have proposed that national GNP and population should be used as the keys, with the relative weights on each to be determined. Alternatively, the seigniorage revenues could be applied to the Community budget.

Which would be better for Ireland from the narrow cash-flow perspective? It may be argued that Ireland will continue to benefit more from the Community budget than would be implied by its share in Community GNP or population.

---

[14]Though terminology varies: some authors preferring to attach the term to the revenues that would accrue only from currency in non-inflationary times, describing the remainder as the 'inflation tax' and the 'reserve requirements tax'.

But this need not mean that Ireland would do better from the ECB seigniorage being transferred to the Community budget, as the consequence might not be a higher level of Community services but a reduction in alternative sources of Community revenue. The formula distribution approach might therefore be seen as a more reliable way of ensuring that the loss of seigniorage from the existing arrangements[15] was made good.

Nevertheless, applying the seigniorage revenues to the Community budget (which would be more in line with practice in federal states such as the US) would have the considerable merit of augmenting what can only be seen in the context of an economic and monetary union as a pitifully inadequate EC budget. It would do so in what would, at least from a political point of view, be a relatively painless way. But this opportunity is likely to be lost as the trend of current thinking seems to favour the formula distribution approach.

[15]The amounts payable to the Government in respect of the Central Bank of Ireland's surplus income in 1989 and 1990 has been close to IR£150 million in each year.

4. LIMITATIONS OF THE MONETARY UNION

Once one moves from the generalities of price stability and an appropriate policy for the trend in bank liquidity, the rosy picture of a smoothly functioning financial system governed from the centre becomes somewhat less sharply focused. In this section, we examine some limitations of monetary union. After briefly noting the problems caused by divergences in fiscal policy, we look at the ability of the EMU to cope with shocks, and specifically asking is the loss of monetary independence likely to lead to serious problems for a country like Ireland? We also discuss the likely evolution of interest rates and financial flows under the EMU.

(i) Fiscal Divergence in the Monetary Union

Though countries with the weakest record of price stability and fiscal discipline have the most go gain from adherence to a monetary union, admitting them could possibly cause problems. Not only might their representatives on the ECB Council weaken the overall anti-inflationary monetary stances of the union but, it has been argued, membership would be taken by the financial markets as an implicit guarantee of the member government's debt. Such problems may have been overstated, especially in view of the built-in independence of the ECB already discussed, and the surveillance of budgetary deficits which is to be introduced as part of the EMU.

Indeed excessive government spending financed by deficit is likely to become less attractive for the government because of the likely adverse effect on business and consumer confidence. Recognising that an EMU government with a deficit cannot simply inflate it away by printing money, nationals of a deficit country will be more likely to fear additional future taxation; this will discourage investment and growth, and even encourage emigration of labour and capital.

The ease with which such factor movements can occur in response to actual or feared taxation is, of course, little comfort to countries like Ireland which start with a higher than average level of government expenditure (partly due to very high government debt servicing). Increased economic integration, especially in financial markets, will place extreme pressure on the ability of the Irish government to maintain higher rates of tax in the years ahead. It will require considerable fiscal skills to effect the necessary expenditure moderation, and to adapt tax structures in Ireland that minimise outflows of labour and capital.

As the most mobile factor, and one whose mobility will increase in the immediate future, the taxation of liquid assets presents immediate problems for Ireland. The retention tax on deposit interest was very effective in limiting the budget deficit when it was introduced in 1986, largely by ensuring that income tax already due was paid. At that time it seemed that interest withholding taxes would be introduced across Europe; unfortunately that is no longer the case.[16] Now with the end of exchange controls, and the new freedoms for cross-border banking after 1992, it is likely that receipts from the retention tax will soon drop, whether or not the rate of tax is reduced. Despite the tight (though improved) budgetary situation, the inevitability of this process should be recognised and the rate of tax scaled down by the end of 1992 in order to avoid outflows of deposits.

(ii) Ability of the EMU to Cope with Shocks

We began with the proposition that, microeconomic convenience and efficiency considerations aside, the main argument for a common currency was to remove the whole monetary process from the political sphere so as to eliminate domestic policy biases that could lead to high inflation. But what about the external shocks to which the economies of Europe are subject? How will the common currency cope with these, and can we be sure that the interests of small countries will be adequately covered? The answer to this question hinges partly[17] on the degree of efficiency and sophistication which one attributes to labour and financial markets in Europe.

A distinction may be drawn between the ability of the ECB to cope with shocks that hit all parts of the EMU more or less equally, and its ability to deal with asymmetric shocks benefiting some regions and damaging others. A decline in US import demand might be an example of a fairly symmetric shock, while energy price increases were less symmetric, while the UK remained a net exporter of fuels. For symmetric shocks, the options available to the ECB are no different from those available to the monetary authorities of any large country: monetary expansion or contraction could be managed as appropriate for the whole union. By avoiding beggar-my-neighbour behaviour, a common central bank might even be able to do better in coping with such shocks (Giavazzi and Giovannini, 1990). But for asymmetric shocks which call for qualitatively different responses in different parts of the union the situation is much more difficult. Differential exchange rate movements are ruled out. Furthermore, depending on the degree of capital mobility, attempts to engineer simultaneously a monetary expansion in one part of the union and a contraction elsewhere could be frustrated.

Empirical analysis of the pattern of shocks hitting EC countries finds that, on the whole, symmetric shocks tend to be larger than asymmetric shocks (Cohen and Wyplosz, 1989; Weber, 1990). Furthermore, symmetric shocks are more

[16]Nor does it seem likely that there will be reporting of deposit interest paid to tax authorities on a common basis across Europe.

[17]One's conclusion would also be coloured by whether or not an adequate EC-wide fiscal mechanism was put in place to respond to shocks.

often lasting ones than transitory, while the opposite is true for asymmetric shocks. This provides some comfort for advocates of the EMU, especially as progressive economic integration should reinforce this tendency to symmetry in shocks, in that shocks will tend to be transmitted quickly throughout an integrated Community. But it remains true that asymmetric shocks — even persistent ones — do still occur, and would mainly fall to be dealt with by fiscal measures if there were a single currency.

Ability of monetary policy to influence interest rates

Actually, the ability of monetary policy to cope with shocks can be overstated. In the past, it was usually held that a sufficiently flexible exchange rate regime and an active monetary policy could influence interest rates and competitiveness in a lasting manner.

Though most close observers are willing to accept that monetary policy can still influence short-term interest rates and generate capital inflows or outflows, neither monetary nor exchange rate policy is any longer thought to be able to insulate domestic long-term real interest rates from developments abroad at least for large economies.

Despite the general observation (on which we have been relying) that capital now flows very freely across frontiers in the industrial world, there remain some residual doubts about whether capital flows will respond reliably to excess credit demands in small economies. To be sure, recent experience within the Community (notably the large capital flows into Spain, Portugal and Ireland) has been adduced as an indication of how mobile capital is, especially when perceived exchange rate risk is low. But it is less clear whether these inflows would continue in response to excess credit demand against a background of deteriorating local economic conditions.[18] An ECB could easily find itself in a situation where liquidity was draining out of one region or country because of a generalised loss of investor confidence. It might then have to take special steps to support liquidity on a regional basis, if it judged that the market was not supplying enough for local investment needs. This would clearly require a departure from the market-oriented liquidity management techniques that were discussed above. To what extent this type of special intervention should be anticipated in the design of the EMU is worth considering. Who would make the decision as to a special liquidity intervention? Would it be prudent to rely on the national central bank to make this decision or would that present each small central bank with an incentive to expand liquidity knowing that any inflationary consequences would tend to be diluted by the large common market and

[18]Euphoric capital inflows to Chile in 1978–81, in circumstances not dissimilar to that recently prevailing in Spain, were quickly followed by revulsion.

common currency? Until financial markets throughout Europe can be expected to function as smoothly in transmitting liquidity within the union as do those within the United States, teething problems of this kind may occasionally emerge.

Monetary policy and competitiveness

Surely the main contribution of monetary policy to good economic performance is through the maintenance of a stable price environment. But monetary actions have been used also to deal directly with competitiveness problems. The appropriate role of monetary policy in securing competitiveness has always related more to the short-run, and to offsetting the emergence of competitiveness losses arising from external shocks, or from inflexibility in the wage and price determination in the economy. The need for such actions, and indeed their effectiveness, has depended in all countries on how well the labour market functions to secure real wage levels that are in line with the evolving competitive conditions.

In the 1960s and early 1970s nominal wage rates tended to be inflexible in most European countries. It was then for the monetary authorities to ensure that the general price level did not get out of line with wage rates. Nominal wage rigidity has since become less serious in that trade unions and employers negotiating wage contracts rapidly adapted their behaviour during the inflationary 1970s with the result that the inflexibility or 'stickiness' of nominal wage rates was greatly reduced. Accordingly there is much less need than before for monetary policy to offset inappropriate wage settlements, and indeed it has much less ability to do so. Now it seems that real wages, rather than nominal, are the target of negotiations: attempts by monetary policy to achieve a real wage other than that targeted by the negotiators are less likely to have any lasting success. One's assessment as to the degree to which this shift has occurred determines one's evaluation of the loss of an independent monetary instrument in each country.[19]

Other rigidities prevent European labour markets from being efficient. Mention may be made of a widely discussed theory according to which 'insiders' (e.g. long-established and senior workers) tend to maintain real wages even in the face of an adverse shock at the cost of creating unemployment among newcomers to the firm and otherwise disadvantaging 'outsiders'. Even if these and other rigidities are an important contributory factor in Europe's poor unemployment record in the last twenty years, it is clear that, since they are

---

[19] Some of the UK's fears concerning the EMU derive from a less pessimistic view on the effectiveness of activist monetary policy.

'real' rather than 'nominal' in character, they can hardly be dealt with by monetary policy now, so they do not provide an argument for delaying the abandonment of national autonomy in monetary policy.[20]

Declining belief in the usefulness of activist monetary policy is one of the reasons why EMU has become such an attractive proposition. Still, though greatly overstressed by some, the loss of monetary independence is not wholly costless since, as indicated by our discussion there are types of external shock requiring price and wage adjustments which could best be achieved by a monetary or exchange rate action. Since such actions will hardly be available for shocks affecting one country, such as Ireland, alone, the adjustment costs of that type of shock could be higher under EMU. There could, indeed should, be a compensatory fiscal response. It is clear that much needs to be done to build the necessary institutional arrangements to yield such a fiscal response (this point is taken up in Rory O'Donnell's *The Regional Issue,* the final paper in this book).

(iii) Interest Rates and Financial Flows

Though we will qualify this statement below, it may fairly be said that, because of the elimination of currency risk, and improved competition, it is likely that Irish interest rates will generally be lower in EMU than they would be if Ireland remained outside. But before EMU is completed, other important events will intervene: the removal of outward exchange controls could tend to be a factor increasing interest rates (though some controls at present discourage foreign investment, and there could be some offset from a favourable psychological effect from the removal of controls); while the reduction or elimination (apparently inevitable, as mentioned, given the 1992 process) of the retention tax on deposit interest and the bank levy will tend to lower them. In this section we concentrate on the situation in Stage Three of EMU, leaving transitional issues to Section 5.

It is commonly asserted that, in the full EMU, interest rates will be the same throughout the union. It would be more precise to say that *currency risk* as a source of differences in interest rates will be eliminated. Interest rates differ from one borrower to another for many reasons, including the perceived risk of default and the degree to which the borrower's circumstances are known to lenders, the lender's cost of monitoring the borrower's performance, the degree of competition in the credit market to which the borrower has access and the currency being borrowed. Only the last two of these will clearly be affected by the EMU, and only the last source of difference completely eliminated.

---

[20]For Ireland, the ESRI Medium-Term Model pictures wage bargaining with real wage targets only partly moderated by the existence of unemployment (Bradley, FitzGerald and McCoy, 1991).

Specifically, liquidity and default risk will remain factors for all securities that are traded. Even if Irish government securities are regarded as carrying essentially no default risk, still the thinness of the market in these securities means that they will still have to offer a very slightly higher yield than the lowest available in the market. That was the situation under the sterling link, and it will continue to be the case in the EMU.

It is worth delving more deeply here, to look at factors which are likely to be of secondary importance, but will nevertheless be present. An additional negative factor affecting the yields of Irish government securities is that, since they will no longer be the most liquid assets free of exchange risk available to Irish residents, they will tend to be displaced in Irish portfolios by foreign securities. That is, even if they are no less liquid than before, yet they will have suffered the disadvantage of having been superseded by an even more liquid security. Finally, to the extent that Irish banks at present hold Irish government securities for liquidity purposes, they too may wish to reduce their holdings, replacing them with an instrument which is more widely acceptable as collateral among the foreign banks with whom they will begin to have more important correspondent relationships.

Indeed, the position of Irish banks (and of the banks of other small countries) in regard to the EMU-wide money market is worth considering. At present, though the Dublin interbank market is an active one, the banks still have direct recourse to the Central Bank for supporting their liquidity needs. This support can be very substantial at times.[21] With such heavy reliance on direct borrowing from the Central Bank, there must be some question as to how well the Irish banks will be able to cope with the new regime of monetary policy in the EMU.

At present, monetary policy practice differs widely as between member states (Kneeshaw and Van den Bergh, 1989). Direct lending by the central bank to commercial banks has remained an important element in Belgium, France and the Netherlands, as well as in Spain and the smaller countries, but less so in Germany, Italy and the United Kingdom. Recent indications are that the move to indirect, market-oriented techniques of liquidity support, long the dominant method of support in the UK and US, will accelerate in other European countries.

As already mentioned, it seems clear that this trend toward a market-oriented liquidity management system will continue in the EMU. This will necessarily mean that the individual liquidity needs of different banks will not be the central focus of policy interventions. It is to be expected that, typically, liquidity injections will be by way of the purchase or sale of securities in the market.[22]

---

[21]As recently as December 1990, Central Bank lending to local banks approached £900 million, equivalent to about 6 per cent of bank deposit liabilities. At end-1989 lending was even higher at £1,300 million.

[22]These could be outright purchase, or reversed transactions where there is agreement to buy back the securities sold at a predetermined price.

Especially for a small bank, direct borrowing from the ECB at the initiative of the borrowing bank could become rare. For one thing, a system which relied on bilateral credit relationships with the ECB would be impractical because of the large number of banks. Furthermore, it seems likely that small banks will operate through larger correspondents in accessing the central money market, rather than dealing directly.

The two largest Irish banks lie towards the bottom of the list of 100 largest EC banks. There are only one or two Greek or Portuguese banks in the same list. How will even the main commercial banks in peripheral countries fare in a system of liquidity management operating from the centre? It seems likely that they could suffer some competitive disadvantage of scale. This could compound the existing high cost structure and result in the Irish banks having difficulty in maintaining growth in their deposit base. If foreign banks offer a cheaper range of ancillary services, larger Irish depositors may be lured away to them. The same would apply with even greater force to banks in Greece and Portugal. It is very hard to judge the magnitude of this effect. At present exchange controls still bottle in Irish depositors, as they do in Greece and Portugal. By the end of 1992, the exchange control barrier will be removed and, though the existence of exchange risk will still provide some shelter for local banks inasmuch as Irish depositors will still want deposits denominated in Irish pounds, a large part of the effect will already be seen.[23, 24]

Not only will the shareholders of the banks be hit by these developments,[25] but the small borrower could also suffer. If Irish banks lose market share in deposits, they will have to rely more on securing interbank funds. Because they are known to be sound, the main Irish banks will have access to such funds, but their need to have recourse to funds at money-market interest rates to replace cheaper lost deposits could take its toll in terms of bank profitability and the scale of their lending may be curtailed.[26] Small Irish borrowers may find it hard to obtain funds from banks that do not have local knowledge, so the outflow of funds to risk-free deposits in banks outside the country may not be balanced by a corresponding inflow of lending from foreign banks.

---

[23]With residual protection — pending stage three of EMU — coming from the fact that most foreign banks may not find it worth their while offering Irish pound accounts.

[24]Removal of exchange controls has already begun. A major step was taken in early 1989, freeing most institutional and personal portfolio investment, though constraining localisation rules for insurance company investments remain in effect. Inward portfolio investment was substantially liberalised in March 1990. The remaining important controls to be removed are those on the net open position of banks — though prudential restrictions will remain here — and on the maintenance of bank deposits by residents.

[25]Coming on top of reduced profitability resulting from intensified competition following the completion of the single market.

[26]Importing wholesale funds before the single currency is established will be even more costly in that the banks will be incurring exchange risk.

This effect is hard to quantify, and it may be overstated here. After all, such problems would not occur in a perfectly efficient financial system where all participants had full information; they do not appear to be severe in the US, for example, where most banks obtain their liquidity indirectly from correspondents. Nevertheless, it must be acknowledged as a potential problem, if only a teething problem, arising directly from the establishment of the ECB and its likely approach to monetary policy.

These EMU-induced problems will be additional to the problems of competition likely to be faced by the Irish banks as a result of the 1992 process which will allow foreign banks to offer banking services in Ireland. Although foreign banks are unlikely to sweep through the market (name recognition and local knowledge will remain powerful advantages for the local banks), there is no doubt that the Irish banks will be squeezed by the completion of the single market in banking. While Irish banks have on average tended, until very recently, to be quite profitable by international standards, the high margins they charge have also been attributable to their high cost base. This cost factor obviously needs to be addressed urgently by the banks. As already mentioned, taxes and other impositions on the banking system (including the bank levy and reserve obligations) will also present additional problems for them in competing with newcomers, though this is recognised by the authorities and seems likely to be addressed by government policy in good time.[27]

(iv) EMU and the Sterling Link

Ireland was part of a monetary union with the UK for the first half-century of independence. Some of our projections about the future draw on that experience, notably the common interest rates and the convergence of inflation rates. There are other lessons to be learned, including the minimal ability of the Irish authorities to influence British monetary actions during the Sterling-link period. Despite formal participation in the decision-making bodies of the EMU, it is only realistic to assume that Ireland's independent role in influencing European monetary policy will be little greater under EMU.

Was the sterling link better or worse than alternatives for Ireland? This question will long be debated, and the answer will generally depend on what alternatives one imagines as being available. On the one hand, the convenience of the common currency may well have prolonged excessive reliance on the UK as the only market considered by Irish exporters, and that market was in long-term decline. On the other hand, it is surely no coincidence that the deterioration in Irish budgetary discipline occurred at the same time as acute UK fiscal and

---

[27]Taxation of financial institutions is a complex matter: there are elements in the tax code that favour the banks; the aim should not be to cushion the shareholders of the banks but to enable them to play, as the hackneyed phrase has it, on a level playing field.

monetary problems emerged during the 1970s; fiscal slippage in Ireland had previously been checked abruptly by the external discipline of the currency link.

Paradoxically, Ireland's membership of the EMS with its realignment possibilities proved, at least at first, to be a weak currency option. From 1979, sterling appreciated under the combined effects of higher oil prices and newly-tightened monetary policy. The new exchange rate regime allowed the Irish economy to be sheltered from some (though not all) of the adverse deflationary effects of sterling's appreciation.

The most acceptable conclusion is that a common currency is most beneficial if the dominant partner countries have stable domestic macroeconomic management and a strong growth potential. The EMU presumably offers better prospects in this regard than did the sterling link.

5. TRANSITIONAL ISSUES

This section looks at the question of transition towards the full Third Stage EMU. It begins by describing why interest rates are likely to be higher in the transition than in the full EMU. It goes on to review the various proposals for transitional arrangements on the way to monetary union, including the alternative proposals for the ecu. The speed of transition is also reviewed. As the negotiations continue, it begins to appear that this transition may be a prolonged one in which there will be no common currency, no sanctions for excessive budget deficits, and possibly not even an operational ECB.

(i) Interest Rates in the Transition

It is widely believed that peripheral members of the EMS have experienced higher interest rates because of the exchange risk involved in holding peripheral currencies. The higher local interest rates, forced by market pressures, were unambiguously bad: savers did not really benefit because the higher rates were needed to compensate them for the risks; firms presumably held back from making investments in plant and equipment that might have been worthwhile at the lower interest rates net of this premium being paid for exchange risk. Likewise, the taxpayer suffered from additional distorting taxation required to service high interest rates on domestic government debt.

These high interest rates have been a damaging weakness of the EMS exchange rate system. And they are avoidable: the risks arise from the possibility of future national policy actions which would be ruled out in an unambiguously fixed-rate regime. Some have argued that an unambiguous statement declaring commitment to the existing central rate in the EMS would help reduce perceived exchange risk. And so it may.[28] But the problem is that such statements inevitably fall short of being fully credible. Both speaker and listener know that there are circumstances, however unlikely, under which a further realignment might occur.[29] Only a common currency can completely eliminate exchange risk within Europe.

More recently, the rapid rise in German interest rates, attributable to the high cost of financing East German reconstruction and recovery, has narrowed the differential between German and other EMS currencies. From the position at the beginning of 1990, when French short-term interest rates were about 300 basis points above those in Germany, this FF–DM differential fell to less than 100 basis points by late in 1990, and the two rates had almost converged by the Spring of 1991. Though long-term interest rate differentials (less subject to

---

[28]Last year's announcement by the Belgian National Bank is sometimes held to have had a favourable effect of this type, but it was accompanied by a package of other measures including the abolition of a withholding tax on interest payments.

[29]This is the credibility problem once again.

manipulation by national monetary authorities) also fell, they were still about 50 basis points in mid-1991. Irish interest rates tended to remain some 50 basis points or so above French levels.

Even if the differentials with Germany have narrowed, this does not weaken our argument that the risk of realignments makes the EMS a system which generates higher than necessary interest rates; rather the contrary. The higher German interest rates have occurred for two reasons: the increased demand for loanable funds[30] and the perception of some increased risk of future inflation in Germany from monetary financing of the deficit. If it is not unreasonable to think of an ECB as being able to deliver a currency which would be immune from inflationary threats posed by national fiscal difficulties, then one can argue that ecu interest rates would not have risen by as much as DM rates have done had the ECB and common currency already been in place.[31]

In this view, therefore, the EMS is an unsatisfactory middle ground between a flexible exchange rate regime and the common currency, and gives rise to the argument that every year's delay in implementing the latter is a year in which growth prospects are damaged by excessive interest rates, not only in the peripheral countries, but perhaps also in Germany.

(ii) Transitional Ecus and the Speed of Transition

A fast-track to the single currency

While the ultimate aim of the EMU is to end up with a single currency, the speed of this transition and the nature of the progressive convergence of the existing currencies is as yet quite open. Recall that Portugal and Greece are still outside the exchange rate mechanism of the EMS, that Spain and the UK still avail of wider +/– 6 per cent margins in the EMS and that, while the last realignment of actual significance for market rates was back in January 1987, this very fact means that unresolved tensions arising from loss of competitiveness have built up again and have been masked by a degree of speculative weakness of the DM. All of these factors point to a system of currencies which is far from being tightly convergent. In particular, while all member states participating in the EMS seem firmly committed to avoiding realignments in the future, the reality of the situation is that they may not be able to stick fully to this commitment.

The Delors Report envisaged that a progressive tightening of convergence would occur to the point where the final stage of EMU would take place with hardly any noticeable change in expectations: currencies would already be so tightly cemented together that to replace them by a single currency would

[30]This has been more a result of increased fiscal deficit than of any great surge in private capital formation in East Germany.

[31]Here we move beyond the traditional argument that the peripheral countries are buying German credibility to a claim that better-than-German credibility can be achieved through a single ECB.

merely represent a convenient economy. This is such a gradualist proposal that inevitably, informed by the Delors Report, current plans for Stage Three place it no earlier than 1997, and possibly well into the new century.

In historical practice, the adoption of a new currency has usually been an abrupt and sudden decision resulting from the collapse of the previous currency regime, and representing an attempt to sweep away the expectational legacy of the past. This is not always successful.[32] But, when accompanied by new institutional arrangements (and a clear policy for budgetary discipline), currency reforms have been successful in stabilising both expectations and the reality of inflation.[33] Argentina has effectively adopted the US dollar for most purposes, both currency and banking, since early 1990. Although this has not stemmed local currency inflation, it has provided the Argentine economy and people with a stable medium of exchange. In that case the adoption of a stable, externally-managed currency did not have to await a long process of convergence.

The European inflation experience over the last two decades is much less acute than that of the countries just mentioned, and there is nothing like the same need for a new currency. But by the same token it is arguable that if the hyper-inflationary Argentine economy can cope with the adoption of a wholly new currency, European economies would be able to absorb the transition to EMU even more easily, and in a relatively short timescale. On this argument, five or ten years seems unnecessarily long as a transition period.

The consensus for gradualism that has reportedly built up among the participants in the policy debate may need to be reconsidered. If one were to wait for the Delors convergence, it might never come. External shocks do occur, and the supposed ideal moment, when all economies have settled down to long-run equilibrium, is likely to be elusive. Why not give more active consideration now to a fast-track approach to EMU?

Though it need not be a two-track approach, a fast-track approach, by which we mean reaching Stage Three by, say, 1994 could pose problems for some member states. The UK is conspicuous by its political reluctance to move away from the pound sterling. Portugal and Greece might experience fiscal difficulties because of the loss of seigniorage. But there would be no obvious reason for other countries not to begin Stage Three, with the door being left open for other countries to join when are able to do so.

Objections to a two-track approach can certainly be offered on other, especially political grounds. For one thing, a fast-track might not leave enough time for negotiating the accompanying fiscal measures which would be

---

[32]The introduction of the Israeli sheqel in February 1980 is a conspicuous case in point, as is the series of new currencies introduced in Brazil during the 1980s: Cruzado replacing Cruzeiro (February, 1986), New Cruzado (January, 1989), and Cruzeiro again (March, 1990), each following its predecessor into oblivion, having shrunk to a tiny fraction of its starting value of only months before.

[33]Most famously in Germany in 1923.

desirable. Ireland has a special interest in such accompanying measures, and it could be a tactical error to agree to Stage Three of EMU with an inadequate package. Another point is that, much as the absence of sterling from the EMS created difficulties, an EMU without sterling would be much less attractive for Ireland than one in which the United Kingdom was a full participant.

Some might argue for delaying Stage Three because of their fears concerning the vulnerability of peripheral economies to European integration. But much of this integration is already in progress. It is doubtful whether delaying monetary union would slow it by much.

The hard-ecu and other gradualist alternatives

The other radical alternative to this two-track EMU is the UK proposal for the immediate introduction of a common currency which would compete with, and ultimately displace, national currencies. This is the so-called 'hard-ecu' proposal, though the same term has been used for much less radical transitional proposals. The UK proposal effectively involves much of the institutional changes involved in mainstream plans for EMU but without abandoning national currencies. It is thus similar to the adoption by Argentina of the US dollar alongside the austral. In the UK proposal, a European Monetary Fund (EMF) would issue what we may call 'hecu' notes and coin against receipt of EC currency. The hecu would be legal tender in all member states; it would be a participant currency in the EMS, and all member states would undertake never to appreciate their currencies in a realignment against the hecu.[34] The EMF would manage monetary policy through market interventions in hecu-denominated securities. The expectation of this model is that the hecu, by virtue of its stable value in terms of goods, would begin to attract significant use as a unit of account and a store of value and, as it became more widely used, its usefulness as a means of payment would also increase. This virtuous circle would lead to the hecu ultimately displacing other currencies and becoming *de facto* the sole currency in the Community.

There are risks in the UK proposal. As other currencies become less in demand, their value would tend to become more volatile. Monetary policy in respect of national currencies would become more difficult, and these currencies would become more prone to inflation. Furthermore the circulation of national currencies and hecu side-by-side would certainly be inconvenient for transactions purposes, and thus some of the benefit of a common currency would be foregone.

All in all, though the UK proposal is more likely to work in achieving a displacement of national currencies than its opponents allow, it would do so only

---

[34]Note that the value of the hecu would not be based on a basket of EMS currencies as it is at present.

at a cost. Furthermore, while it might get results more quickly than the somewhat indeterminate timetable now emerging from the gradualist Delors Report approach, it is hard to see what it offers ahead of a fast-track EMU to those committed to monetary union.

Other proposals for the ecu in the transitional stage are much more narrowly focused and should not be confused with the radical UK proposal. None of them have much more than technical significance.

The German and French idea is that there should be an agreement to reweight the basket defining the value of the ecu at any realignment in order to ensure that it passes through the realignment without any depreciation against a member currency. This proposal does not call for ecu currency, legal tender status, or for a monetary fund. Furthermore, it is not unambiguously clear that the change would promote the use of the ecu as an unit of account in international financial transactions and assets. While it would be likely to make the value of the ecu more stable in terms of goods, by making it the strongest currency instead of an average of the EMS currencies, it would tend to destabilise its value against a typical national EMS currency.

An alternative idea is that the basket weights of the ecu should not be adjusted from now on.[35] The implication of not reweighting the basket is that if there are realignments, and if some currencies are systematically weaker than others at these realignments, then over time the ecu could become stronger than it would become under present procedures. On the other hand the percentage share taken by the stronger currencies would grow and that of the weaker currencies would shrink over time.[36]

(iii) The Changeover

Assuming that the UK proposal is not adopted, how will the changeover to the new ecu occur and what are the potential problems? It is worth bearing in mind that, though the new issues of currency will be the most colourful aspect of the changeover, the adoption of the ecu as the local currency in each country will involve a redefinition of all financial claims and obligations in terms of ecu. Thus if the changeover rate of exchange is determined to be, say IR£1 = 1.3 ecu, then mortgage service payments of, say, IR£212.73 will automatically become payments of 276.55 ecu as determined by law. The Irish pound debt of the government will become an ecu-denominated debt, and so on.

---

[35]Up to now there have been periodic adjustments of the basket. The total value of the basket has not been changed at these adjustments, but the percentage share in the basket of each currency has been brought back to an agreed figure from which it may have drifted because of realignments.

[36]Actually these effects are really very small. The original 1979 ecu would now be worth £0.782 compared with its actual value of £0.768 — a difference of only 2 per cent.

Probably the closest analogy we have is the experience of decimal day in 1971, but in that case only quantities of less than one pound were affected.[37] Furthermore, although the conversion rate between new and old pence was not exactly a round number (1p = 2.4d) in practice several of the more important old coins could be retained as they represented a round number of new pence (10p = 24d = 2s; 5p = 12d = 1s).[38] No such convenient multiples can be anticipated for the ecu changeover. As was the case following decimal day, the old notes and coin will be withdrawn promptly as they reach the banking system, and a deadline will be imposed after which the old notes are no longer legal tender, though they may still be encashed by special presentation at a bank, and eventually only at the Central Bank.

There will undoubtedly be scope for much confusion and even exploitation of simple or elderly people in the matter of restating prices in ecu. This will be similar to the experience of travellers in foreign countries at present and, while it does not pose insurmountable problems, will undoubtedly involve considerable short-term disruption no matter how well it is planned.

A significant open question concerning the start-up arrangements relates to the transfer of national foreign exchange reserves to the European Central Bank. The sums involved are appreciable: total EC reserves, less gold, amount to something of the order of 200 billion ecu. The ECB will naturally need to have foreign exchange reserves at its disposal for the purpose of intervening in foreign exchange markets to sell third currencies. Presumably, its stock will be built up through a transfer of existing reserves from national authorities. How many reserves should be transferred? One key could be that reserves transferred should be equal to the amount of currency converted. To insist on all reserves being handed over would appear on the one hand to be unfair to those countries now holding relatively large sums and on the other to be likely to lead to a scramble to divest oneself of reserves.[39, 40]

---

[37]Another analogy worth recalling in this connection is the switch to selling petrol by the litre, and other metrication changes.

[38]As did the ten-shilling note, replaced with the 50p piece.

[39]The swap procedures at present used for the partial transfer of reserves under EMS are so artificial and indeed almost fictitious that they cannot serve the more real purposes intended for the ECB.

[40]It will also be important to ensure that the time of year chosen for the changeover set does not disadvantage some countries. The ECB will be assuming responsibility for all of the national currencies outstanding at the time of changeover, so the more of one's currency is issued, the better. The difference between peak and trough of currency holdings in a single year in Ireland is some £200 million, and could be even higher under certain circumstances.

6. CONCLUDING REMARKS

Monetary union in Europe will have advantages of convenience and stability which are likely to outweigh the loss of monetary independence. The ability of activist monetary policy to influence output and employment is less now than it was thought to be in the past. Therefore, although price stability will be the central objective of the European Central Bank, that need not imply that employment will be sacrificed. Indeed, a stable macroeconomic environment should be conducive to investment and growth supportive of employment.

It is important, however, that the union should be set-up in such a way as to make the most of the potential gains. In the specifically monetary sphere, this includes severely limiting the residual autonomy of national central banks, if any. The ultimate responsibility for prudential supervision of banks should also be transferred to the European Central Bank.

The Irish banking system, like that in other small countries, will have its work cut out to remain competitive in the new regime. Action by the banks to reduce their costs will need to be complemented by government policy to ensure that local banks are not disadvantaged relative to banks from partner countries. Increased competition facing that and other financial sectors in the years ahead probably derives more from the completion of the single market and from the elimination of exchange controls than from the single currency *per se,* and could be especially acute during the transition.

The present exchange rate regime almost guarantees higher interest rates in Ireland than could be achieved under EMU. For this reason we have argued that it is in Ireland's interest that the transition to the single currency should be brief.

BIBLIOGRAPHY

Bradley, J., J. FitzGerald and D. McCoy, *ESRI Medium-Term Review: 1991–1996,* Dublin, 1991.

Cohen, D. and C. Wyplosz, "The European Monetary System: An Agnostic Evaluation", in R. C. Bryant and others, eds., *Macropolicies in an Interdependent World,* Washington, DC: Brookings, 1989.

Eichengreen, B., "One Money for Europe? Lessons from the US Currency Union", *Economic Policy,* 1990.

Giavazzi, F. and A. Giovannini, "The Role of the Exchange-Rate Regime in a Disinflation: Empirical Evidence on the EMS", in F. Giavazzi, S. Micossi and M. Miller, eds., *The European Monetary System,* Cambridge University Press, 1990.

Giavazzi, F. and M. Pagano, "The Advantage of Tying One's Hands: EMS Discipline and Central Bank Credibility", *European Economic Review,* 1988.

Kneeshaw, J. T. and P. Van den Bergh, "Changes in Central Bank Money Market Operating Procedures in the 1980s", *BIS Economic Papers, No. 23,* Basle, 1989.

Kydland, F. E. and E. C. Prescott, "Rules Rather than Discretion: The Inconsistency of Optimal Plans", *Journal of Political Economy,* 1977.

Lindbeck, A. and D. J. Snower, "Long-Term Unemployment and Macroeconomic Policy", *American Economic Review,* 1988.

National Economic and Social Council (NESC), *Ireland in the 1990s,* Dublin, 1990.

Rogoff, K., "The Optimal Degree of Commitment to an Intermediate Monetary Target", *Quarterly Journal of Economics,* 1985.

US Office of the Comptroller of the Currency, "Bank Failure: An Evaluation of the Factors Contributing to the Failure of National Banks", Washington, DC, 1988.

Weber, A., "EMU, Asymmetries and Adjustment Problems in the EMS", *CEPR Discussion Paper, No. 448,* 1990.

THE REGIONAL ISSUE

Rory O'Donnell

EXECUTIVE SUMMARY

The Issue of Cohesion in the Community System

One of the objectives of the Community is the creation of 'economic and social cohesion' and, in the EC, the word cohesion is frequently used to refer to the problems of social and regional inequalities.

While the Treaty of Rome was primarily addressed to the task of creating a common market, it recognised the existence of regional problems and, to a degree, sacrificed the common market to regional and other objectives. However, the common market was sacrificed, not for other *Community* objectives and policies, but for national, regional and industrial policy aims.

Despite considerable development of Community regional and social policy, the original Treaty formulation has shaped these policies and the place of the cohesion question in the overall Community system. Community social and regional policies were, and largely remain, national policies part-funded by the EC. Member states remain free to pursue regional and social policies which may cut across the Community cohesion objective. Although the cohesion was a stated Community objective, its pursuit through national instruments meant that it was not taken into account in the main body of Community policies.

The issues of monetary union and cohesion have traditionally been closely linked in political and economic discussion within the Community (see below). In very recent years this link has been weakened, mainly for political reasons, and an attempt was made to keep the cohesion issue out of the 1991 Treaty negotiations on EMU.

Limited progress on political union, and climate of opinion which this reflects, conditioned the concrete Treaty proposals on cohesion at the 1991 Inter Governmental Conferences. The main Treaty change is the insertion of the requirement that the Commission report every three years on progress towards cohesion and, where necessary, make proposals for action by the Community and the member states.

Deciding on EMU: The Argument in Outline

An influential viewpoint states that it is the monetary stage of integration which can particularly exacerbate regional problems — because the impossibility of exchange rate devaluation will expose regions to the employment and output effects of economic disturbances. This view of the regional effects of integration needs to be revised for two reasons. First, the regional effects of *earlier* stages of *economic* integration — trade and international mobility of capital and labour — are not so benign as was once believed. Second, for small, very open, countries the loss of the exchange rate instrument is not as significant as suggested in the traditional argument.

Therefore, cohesion considerations provide no compelling general argument against EMU. Indeed, when we consider *policies* which can promote cohesion we find that these could be more substantial and more effective in an advanced stage of integration, such as EMU, than in a common market.

Regional Tendencies in an Economic Union

There are considerable forces making for concentration of advanced economic activity. Economies of scale, economies of agglomeration, advantageous labour market characteristics and innovation leadership tend to provide leading firms in developed, central, populous regions with self-sustaining advantages.

In these circumstances the opening of trade, or capital and labour mobility, will tend to generate large benefits and costs which will be distributed unequally between regions and countries. Nevertheless, it is highly likely that a country like Ireland has gained, in *absolute* terms, from economic integration and will gain, in absolute terms, from further integration.

The existence of a tendency to concentration of economic activity does not imply that this is an *inevitable* outcome and that the fortunes of the centre and the periphery must diverge. First, there are some forces making for diffusion of activity, especially manufacturing. Second, although regional development remains highly uneven there is, in fact, a *shifting hierarchy* of leading and lagging regions. Factors *indigenous* to a region or country — such as political and social structures and economic policies — can influence which peripheral region becomes rich and which leading regions lose their dominance.

The effects of *market forces* in shaping the regional pattern of activity across regions and states is likely to be roughly the same in EMU as at present. Many of the most important forces making for regional convergence and divergence are inseparable from the internationalisation of economic activity which exists independently of the fact that countries embark on formal integration.

These arguments take the emphasis off *monetary* union as the stage of integration which generates problems for weaker regions.

However, it is incorrect to infer from this that the traditional connection between EMU and the cohesion issue no longer has any analytical foundation. EMU will further free the economic forces which shape the regional pattern of activity. In addition, by deepening the integration of markets for goods, services and capital, EMU will further constrain a wide range of national policies — for example, taxation. This could be harmful to both cohesion and the single market and provides a reason why the move to EMU should be accompanied by an extension of the scope of Community policy, including enhanced policies for cohesion.

Regional Aspects of Monetary Union

For a country such as Ireland, exchange rate devaluation provides a limited ability to protect output and employment from the adverse economic developments. Therefore, monetary union can provide at least as good a macroeconomic environment as EMS or floating exchange rates.

However, the creation of a unified financial area will give greater freedom to the forces making for flows of capital between regions. Given the underlying economic differences between regions, there is no guarantee of a uniform availability of finance.

The problems which exchange rate devaluation was intended to address will still exist in EMU. The issue is to devise policies, at both national and Community level, which can solve them.

Policies for Cohesion in EMU

The analysis of regional development and of international trade suggests that indigenous factors — including policies across a wide range — can have significant impact on the prospects of a peripheral region in a economic union.

The development of domestic policy is important, not only because of its impact on economic prospects, but also because it greatly enhances the case for, and belief in, effective Community policies for cohesion.

Although structural measures, coordination of macroeconomic policy and differential application of other Community policies (as provided for in Article 130b) are necessary for cohesion, much the greatest Community contribution to cohesion is likely to arise from the development of the Community budget which will occur when the Community develops its fiscal union. The case for a more developed fiscal union is based on *efficiency* considerations (the implications and requirements of genuine market integration) as well as on *equity* or regional concerns.

A significant change in the place of the cohesion issue in the Community, and significant enhancement of cohesion-promoting Community policies, requires a change in the relationship between the Community and the member states. This is a conclusion which emerges from three independent lines of enquiry: (i) examination of the Community as a political system; (ii) analysis of the requirements and implications of economic integration and (iii) study of what policies are most likely to reduce regional disparities.

In general, progress on Community policies for *economic and social cohesion* is closely related to, and dependent on, development of political cohesion. The current Treaty revision is likely to produce a modest deepening of political integration. This has limited the amount of progress which has been achieved on the cohesion issue.

However, the new requirement for a tri-annual review of the cohesion question ensures that the issue will remain on the political agenda and suggests that attention should soon move from the Treaty design of EMU to the political process. If that process leads to a *further* Treaty revision, in some years time, then the question of cohesion in the Treaty will again become relevant.

If the objective of regional and social cohesion is to be established as a higher Community priority, two things are necessary. First, Ireland must make a leading contribution to the analysis of regional problems and the formulation of cohesion policies. Second, the importance and feasibility of effective common policies for cohesion must be advocated not only at the European Council, the Commission, and in the Parliament but also *in the wider society,* in the same way that the single market programme became an imperative which the Council could not ignore.

1. INTRODUCTION

This paper considers the possible implications of Economic and Monetary Union (EMU) for Ireland's relative social and economic position in the Community. In recent years the term 'cohesion' has come to denote the Community's objective of reducing spatial and social disparities in living standards, employment and unemployment. This term should be distinguished from the word 'convergence', which tends to be used to refer to convergence of economic magnitudes such as inflation rates and interest rates. Although some real magnitudes, such as balance of payments deficits and government budget deficits, are also included in these comparisons, 'convergence' has come, more and more, to denote what might be called 'nominal convergence'. Sometimes the term 'real convergence' is used to refer to convergence of living standards, etc., but to minimise confusion, the word 'cohesion' is used in this paper.

Section 2 examines the place of cohesion, as an objective and a political issue, in the Community system. This involves an identification of regional concerns in the Treaty of Rome and explanation of the subsequent development of Community regional policy. This investigation leads to an assessment of cohesion in the Community system. This suggests, first, that the relationship of the cohesion objective to the common market objective is a reflection of the relationship between the Community and the member states. Evaluation of the Community's structural policies shows that they have achieved limited narrowing of regional disparities since 1975.

Section 3 considers the place of the cohesion issue in the 1991 Inter Governmental Conferences (IGCs) and in the current design and construction of EMU. This reveals that the cohesion issue has been somewhat sidelined in recent discussion of EMU — in comparison with analyses and debate on EMU in the late 1960s and 1970s. I next examine the proposals on cohesion at the 1991 IGC. I compare the submissions of the Irish and Spanish governments, identify the Commission's response, and report the main changes on cohesion in the new Treaty (as drafted by the Luxembourg Presidency in June, 1991).

The economic laws governing the regional pattern of economic activity and income in a European economic and monetary union are considered in Section 4. The analysis is structured around a discussion of one influential view of the regional effects of EMU. The view in question is one which suggests that the problems for weaker regions are most likely to arise at the *monetary* stage of integration. In order to assess this view I discuss separately the regional tendencies in an *economic* union and the regional aspects of *monetary* union. I suggest an alternative perspective on the pattern and timing of the overall costs and benefits of integration for weaker regions. This perspective takes the emphasis off monetary union as the step which raises problems for weaker economies.

Finally, in Section 5, the issues arising for Ireland and the Community are considered. The first issue for the Irish government and people to decide is their overall attitudes to EMU. I discuss how the economic arguments of Section 4 might be used in making a decision for, or against, EMU. These economic analyses suggests that cohesion considerations provide no compelling argument against EMU, and that, on certain conditions, cohesion is more likely to be achieved in an advanced stage of economic, monetary and political integration than in the current situation. The remaining issues concern the approach to the cohesion question which should be adopted in Ireland and at Community level. I argue that the Structural Funds have a definite, but limited, ability to achieve cohesion. This reflects not only the limited resources available but also the limits of current knowledge of the nature and processes of regional development. These arguments and a study of existing federations suggest that the inter-regional distributive mechanisms of a central budget can play a most significant role in the reduction of regional economic disparities. An important political condition for this development is identified — the need for significant 'political homogeneity' on political cohesion.

In assessing the treatment of cohesion in the current phase of design of EMU it is argued that, despite the changed view of the significance of exchange rate movements, there are new analytical arguments which link cohesion to EMU and which suggest that movement to EMU should be accompanied by enhancement of policies which assist cohesion. These arguments derive from developments in the economics of integration which have heightened understanding of the degree to which genuine economic integration constrains national economic policies across a wide spectrum. This new understanding of the integration of mixed economies reveals close connections between economic, monetary, fiscal and political integration.

Irish discussion of the 1991 IGCs and the new Treaty is bound to focus, to some extent, on the somewhat different approaches adopted by the Irish and Spanish governments. Some considerations which should inform any such discussion are identified. Finally, I argue that advance of the cohesion issue requires activity at both the political and analytical levels. The political case for enhanced Community policies will be strengthened if certain fundamental questions about cohesion can be answered. These questions concern the relationship between regional and social inequality, the most effective approach to regional policy and, particularly in Ireland's case, the nature and significance of peripherality. Pursuit of these questions implies, by definition, a rejection of any notion that progress on the cohesion issues consists in, or is measured by, Ireland's net budgetary receipts from the Community.

In evaluating the costs and benefits of EMU it is necessary to adopt three criteria: the regional distribution of production and income; microeconomic performance and management; and, macroeconomic performance and management. It should be noted that this paper is concerned primarily with the likely *regional* distribution of production and income at various stages of economic integration. Consequently, there are many benefits, and some costs, of EMU which are not considered in this paper — an example would be the microeconomic benefit of lower transaction costs. This benefit would only be of concern in this paper if it were likely to be very much larger, or smaller, in Ireland than in other regions of the Community. Other sections of this book — and ongoing studies at the Institute of European Affairs — consider the microeconomic and macroeconomic costs and benefits to Ireland in greater detail. An overall evaluation of EMU requires that the analysis of this complete series of issues be considered jointly.

2. COHESION IN THE COMMUNITY SYSTEM

(i) Introduction

This section provides background information on the place of what is now called the cohesion question in the Community system. The concern here is not with the economic laws governing regional inequalities but with the place which regional and, to a lesser extent, social issues occupy in the political system of the Community. It is most important that Irish discussion and analysis of policy options be based on a realistic view of where the cohesion question fits in the overall objectives and policies of the Community.

(ii) Regional Concerns in the Treaty of Rome

Three Kinds of Reference to the Regional Issue

Although the Treaty of Rome made no provision for a Community regional policy, three different kinds of reference to regional problems can be identified. These are: first, implicit references to regional problems and regional objectives; second, derogations from the general rules governing the common market; third, references to Community methods and instruments which were intended to reduce regional and social inequalities.

The implicit references to regional problems and regional goals can be found in the main statement of the Community objectives. The Preamble to the Treaty included a declaration that the contracting parties were:

> . . . anxious to strengthen the unity of their economies and to ensure their harmonious development by reducing the differences existing between the various regions and the backwardness of the less favoured regions.

Article 2 repeats this objective and states explicitly that the Community shall have among its tasks "a continuous and balanced expansion". In addition, a Protocol concerning Italy, attached to the Treaty, makes reference to Italian efforts to address the regional imbalance in the Italian economy, and recognises that "it is in their common interest that the objectives of the Italian programme should be attained".

Regional concerns are evident in articles referring to agriculture, social and transport policy and, in particular, in articles which stipulate *derogations* from the general Treaty provisions governing the common market. The most significant of these is Article 92, relating to aids granted by member states. The Article lays down that aid which distorts competition is incompatible with the common market, but immediately introduces significant derogations. In particular, the following are said to be compatible with the common market: (a) aid to promote the economic development of areas where the standard of living is abnormally low or where there is serious unemployment; (b) aid to promote the execution of an important project of common European interest or to remedy a serious disturbance in the economy of a member state; (c) aid to facilitate the development of certain economic activities or of certain economic areas, where such aid does not adversely affect trading conditions to an extent contrary to the common interest.[1] Article 92 suggests that the original role of the Community in the area of regional policy was to be largely negative, i.e., the Commission would monitor and vet national aids to industry, but would not be actively involved in regional policy.

However, the Treaty of Rome did establish some Community methods and instruments which undoubtedly have the aim of addressing social and regional inequalities. The European Social Fund was established to address employment problems and gradually acquired a regional function as well (Article 123). Article 128 calls for a common vocational training policy capable of contributing to "harmonious development". Much the most significant regional instrument created by the Treaty of Rome was the European Investment Bank (Article 130). In addition, Article 56 of the 1951 Treaty of Paris, establishing the European Coal and Steel Community (ECSC), provided that, if the establishment of the common market, the introduction of new technologies or fundamental changes in market conditions, led to large redundancies then the common institution (called the High Authority) and/or the member states may provide loans or grants to convert the industries or establish new, economically-sound, activities.

Interpreting the Place of Cohesion in the Treaty

The significance of these various Treaty references to regional issues would seem to be the following. From the start, the Community recognised the existence of regional problems and had among its objectives harmonious development by reducing regional disparities. However, it is important to correctly assess the meaning of this recognition and the nature of this objective. We may first note that the recognition of regional problems was primarily a recognition of the regional problems facing *member states*. In addition, the objective of reducing regional disparities was articulated in very little detail compared to the Community's main concrete objective, the creation of a common market, or compared to the objectives of the main common policies which were viewed as necessary for its creation (competition, commercial, transport, agriculture and social). It would be incorrect, however, to infer from this that the relationships between the two objectives was simply that the efficiency objective of a common market was uniformly given precedence over the regional objective, and that this reflects a general feature of the Community as a *laissez faire* project. The extensive derogations in Article 92 and elsewhere show *that even in the Treaty* — let alone in practice — the common market was

---

[1]See also Articles 39 (2) a; 42a; 49d; 75; 80 (2) and 82.

frequently sacrificed to regional and other objectives. The key point, however, is that the common market was sacrificed, not for other *Community* objectives and policies, but for *national,* regional and industrial policy aims. In short, the relationship between the Community's regional (cohesion) objective and its other objectives cannot be described by examining only *Community-level* Treaties, documents and instruments. The relationship between the regional objective and, say, the common market objective, was tied up with, and a product of, the relationship between Community objectives, policies and institutions, on the one hand, and national objectives, policies and institutions, on the other. These observations are important not only for understanding the development of Community regional policy but also for interpreting, and evaluating, the new Treaty.

(iii) The Development of Community Regional Policy

The Treaty articles discussed above were, and to a considerable extent remain, the basis of regional actions at the Community level. Within this Treaty context, three factors served to promote the development of Community regional policy. First, with the removal of tariffs and quotas the six member states increased their use of regional supports. Second, in the late sixties and early seventies there was an attempt to launch a move to economic and monetary union. Third, the enlargement of 1973 highlighted the degree of regional disparities within the Community. Each of these is now briefly explained.

The Commission's Role

From the early 1960s the Commission worked to analyse regional problems, to gain some control over — or at least knowledge of — national regional supports and to integrate regional issues into the Community's medium-term economic policy.[2] In 1968, a Directorate General for regional policy was created. In fact, it was a fusion of the former administrative units of the EEC Commission and of the ECSC High Authority. The proliferation of national regional supports was doubly damaging to the achievement of a common market because the impact of regional aids on international competition becomes greater with the abolition of trade barriers. It is widely recognised that the Commission has, by and large, faced enormous difficulty in trying to monitor and control national regional supports, although some progress can be reported in recent years.

Plans for Economic and Monetary Union

In the late 1960s, there was a series of proposals on the establishment of EMU and, for reasons that will emerge presently, this served to promote the discussion of Community regional policy. The Werner Report, adopted by the Council in

---

[2]Vanhove and Klaassen (1987) provide a blow-by-blow account of the emergence of Community regional policy in Chapter 10 of their textbook on regional policy.

1971, strongly suggested that the continuation of regional disparities could prevent the attainment of EMU. Indeed, a series of reports and studies during the 1970s argued that monetary union, on its own, could exacerbate the problems of weaker regions and emphasised that when the Community moved to EMU it would require more developed policies to ensure cohesion. The analytical basis of this link between monetary union and regional problems and policies is discussed in Section 4, below. As a result of this link the progress of the cohesion objective came, for many years, to be linked to the issue of EMU and, more broadly, to the degree of ambition of the Community. It is for this reason that one found many documents on the Community saying that the scope of Community regional policy and, more generally, the fate of redistributive politics in the Community is dependent on the move from a common market to an economic and monetary union (see MacDougall, 1977; Laffan, 1984). In very recent years this link between the cohesion issue and monetary union has been weakened, mainly for political reasons, such that the Commission could suggest that the cohesion issue be excluded from the 1991 Inter Governmental Conference on EMU. However, it is important that the role of EMU in the development of Community regional policy not be forgotten. Later, I argue that there are still good reasons to consider EMU and cohesion together.

The Enlargement of 1973

Together with the plans for EMU, the enlargement of the Community in 1973 to include the United Kingdom, Ireland and Denmark provided an important stimulus to the development of Community regional policy. Although the Paris summit of 1972 (which Irish, British and Danish leaders attended) stated that "high priority should be given to the aim of correcting in the Community, the structural and regional imbalances which might affect the realisation of economic and monetary union", and called for a regional fund by the end of 1973, there was, in fact, great resistance by some member states when it came to it. Among other difficulties, it has been argued that "the abandonment of commitment to economic and monetary union in the foreseeable future deprived the Commission of one of its trump cards in the argument for rapid establishment of the Regional Development Fund" (Vanhove and Klaassen, 1987, p. 403). After difficult and protracted negotiations, a Community regional policy came into being with the establishment of the European Regional Development Fund (ERDF) in 1975.

Main Features of Community Regional Policy

The Community's regional policies have developed along three main lines: first, the coordination of the national regional policies of member states to ensure their conformity with the Treaties; second, an attempt to make other Community policies and financing instruments more sensitive to regional disparities; third, the establishment of specific Community regional policy instruments. The content of the policy agreed under these three headings in 1975 was the outcome of a negotiation process and, given that this process has continued, there has been considerable development in the policy since then.

The main features of Community regional policy at its inception were the following:

- the small scale of the ERDF relative to the total Community budget or Community GDP
- the distribution of the ERDF money on the basis of fixed national quotas which ensured that all member states received some support whatever the level of national prosperity
- reliance on *national* determination of regions eligible for support and design of approaches to regional problems.

These aspects of the policy meant that its effectiveness in removing regional disparities was severely limited. Both the Commission and the Parliament identified the limitations of Community regional policy and created consistent and partially successful pressure for change.

To overcome these problems, the Commission has, since 1975, put forward many proposals for reform of the ERDF. These proposals are worth stating since they have set the direction, if not the exact path, in which Community regional policy has moved in a series of reforms — the latest of which was completed in 1989. The changes proposed by the Commission included the following:

- the Commission should have a more active role in regional policy
- the role of set national quotas should be reduced and more of the ERDF should be distributed according to Community rather than national priorities
- funds should be allocated to development *programmes* rather than *projects*
- the regional impact of other Community policies should be monitored and taken into account
- regional development programmes should be 'integrated' — by which it meant that the various Community structural and financial instruments, together with national and sub-national resources, be used in a coordinated way.

The Single Act and After

The most significant reform of Community regional policy was that which followed the revision of the Treaty in the Single Act (1987). This Act not only provided mechanisms to ensure the completion of the single market but also made provisions to address some of the regional tensions which could arise from more intense competition and greater mobility of labour and capital.

The Act strengthened the Community's objective (previously in the Preamble to the Treaty of Rome) of reducing disparities between regions (Article 130a). It specified the ERDF as an instrument designated to this task (up to then the Regional Fund did not have explicit status in the Treaty). Article 130b called for the cohesion objective to be taken into account in the implementation of Community policy. The Single Act also instructed the Commission to submit a comprehensive proposal to the Council concerning amendments to the Structural Funds which would clarify their tasks and increase their effectiveness in reducing disparities (Article 130d).

In August 1987, the Commission presented the Council with its view on how the Structural Funds could be made more effective; it proposed that they should be doubled by 1993. It argued that the resources should be concentrated on a set of five specified objectives, which would focus the funds on areas most in need of support. It envisaged a more active role for the Commission in the design and implementation of structural policies. Regional development *plans* and programmes, rather than individual projects, were specified as the main measures to be submitted to and funded by the Commission. Finally, the Commission advocated that the different levels of government should all be involved in the preparation, financing, monitoring and assessment of development programmes.

It will be recognised immediately that these proposals were not new. They reflect the Commission's long-standing views about reform of Community regional policy. Once again, these proposals proved controversial in the Council of Ministers and once again the outcome was a compromise between the Commission, member states supporting most of its proposals and member states who, at least at present, see a minor role for Community structural policy in reducing regional disparities in Europe.

(iv) Assessing Cohesion in the Community System

Cohesion Policies Equals Structural Funds

Despite the significant effects of other Community policies on social and regional disparities, and the provisions of Article 130b, the question of cohesion has largely come to be identified with the Community's structural policies and, in particular, with the Structural Funds. Given the failure of the Structural Funds to achieve convergence, it is ironic that this identification of cohesion with the Structural Funds has been encouraged not only by those who wish to limit the

Community's role in cohesion but also by member states with severe regional problems. One of the most important requirements for the achievement of greater cohesion is that this identification of the cohesion issue with the Structural Funds be challenged at both the Community and national levels. Nevertheless, given this identification, evaluation of existing Community cohesion policies boils down to evaluation of the success and potential of the Structural Funds.

The Nature of Community Structural Policy

The Community has now had three sets of structural policies in operation for a considerable time. The social policy is aimed at improving the employment opportunities and working conditions of Community citizens. Payments from the European Social Fund, established by the 1957 Treaty of Rome, are used to fund training and retraining of workers whose skills are inadequate due to industrial change, regional problems or social disadvantage. The agricultural guidance policy is intended to address the structural problems in the agriculture sector and is funded by the Guidance Section of the Community's agricultural fund, EAGGF — also established in 1957. The fund provides grants to improve the productivity and structure of farm businesses, to assist investment in food and fish processing facilities and to provide some direct income support in disadvantaged areas. Finally, the regional policy involves grants for infrastructural and industrial projects in less prosperous regions of the Community and is funded by the ERDF, established in 1975. Although most ERDF money has, in all countries, been spent on infrastructure, especially transport infrastructure, there has, in recent years, been a move into new areas. In particular, a set of measures known as Community 'initiatives' are attempting to foster regional development through improving telecommunications, technology, research and development, energy supply, the environment and local economic initiative.

One very important feature that the three Structural Funds have in common is their small size relative to the total Community budget, relative to total Community GDP and, most significantly, relative to the scale of inequalities and structural problems in the European economy. In Table 1, it can be seen that the Community budget has only recently passed 1 per cent of the GDP of the 12 member countries. The Community budget has been, and remains, dominated by agricultural outlays — spent mainly on buying up unwanted food and subsidising exports to the world food market. This accounts for the small share of the Structural Funds in the budget. The European Council, meeting at Brussels in early 1988, agreed a doubling of the Structural Funds by 1993, at which time they will comprise about 25 per cent of the Community budget and 0.3 per cent of Community GDP.

Table 1

The Community Budget and Structural Funds

Year	EC Budget as % of Community GDP	S.F. as % Community Budget	S.F. as % of Community GDP
1972	0.56	4.1	0.02
1980	0.83	15.0	0.12
1986	0.97	16.3	0.16
1989	1.04	19.2	0.20
1993	1.20	25.0	0.30

Evaluating Community Structural Policy

There are great difficulties in evaluating the success of Community structural policies in overcoming obstacles to regional development or narrowing the differences between incomes and life chances in the Community. Some of these difficulties are general and these should be noted. First, all attempts to evaluate structural interventions face the, virtually insurmountable, problem of disentangling the effects of the policy from the other forces which are influencing the regions in question. This is especially acute since structural measures can only be expected to influence the regional pattern of economic activity in the medium-to-long run. Second, regional policy in most western countries, including the EC, is going through a period of turbulence, with a breakdown of consensus, associated with a loss of faith in the effectiveness of the two main approaches in the post-war period — infrastructural investment and attraction of mobile projects by means of capital grants. This means that methods of evaluation devised for conventional post-war regional policy may have to be revised. In addition, since a wide range of projects are now included in regional policy it is not yet clear what we should look for from the new generation of policy approaches. All of these considerations suggest that evaluation of Community structural policy will remain difficult.

These *general* problems of evaluation are compounded by specific features of the Community. First, Community regional and structural policies are still, to a considerable extent, *national* policies part-funded by Community money. This inevitably means that member states apply somewhat different evaluation and auditing procedures to Community money than they do to measures funded from national taxation. Second, and related to this, in the case of some member states, there are doubts as to whether Community Structural Funds result in much additional structural intervention in the designated regions. A third factor which makes evaluation extremely difficult is what Padoa-Schioppa has called "tokenism" in the scale of intervention in the Community's regional and social policies (Padoa-Schioppa, 1987). But Community interventions are small in another sense which also hampers evaluation; they are small relative to the supports, aids and incentives undertaken by most member states — including the most wealthy ones (see Commission, 1990a). Fourth, in the case of the Community, among the 'other' factors influencing the outcome are certain Community policies which have a marked regional impact — the most important of which is probably the CAP.

In spite of these difficulties of evaluation it has to be said that the questions of evaluation, value for money and auditing are extremely important ones in the overall development and status of the cohesion issue in the Community system.

Limited Regional Convergence Since 1975

Despite the complicating factors listed above, evaluation of Community policies for cohesion must begin by assessing the extent to which national and regional disparities have actually been reduced. In studying the evolution of income levels in the member states from 1960 to 1989, the Commission has identified two phases. Up until around 1973–4 there was an unmistakable process of convergence; since the mid-1970s there has been a reversal. The disparity between income levels of the Twelve fell considerably until 1973–4. Much of this was the result of very strong growth in Spain, Portugal and Greece between 1960 and 1970 — though these countries were not members of the Community during that period. By and large, disparities between *regional* income levels followed a similar pattern — though the narrowing of disparities in the early period was fairly limited. The turnaround from convergence to divergence was even more marked when unemployment rates are considered.

Other studies have measured not only regional and unemployment levels but also regional economic structures as revealed by the pattern of industry, agriculture, services and demography. One such study, by Keeble, Owens and Thompson (1982), revealed significant and *widening* differences between the economic structure of central and peripheral regions in Europe in the period 1965 to 1979. A later study showed some convergence in industrial structures in the 1980s. Both these studies suggest that, in comparison with the southern European periphery, Ireland's industrial structure has been considerably 'modernised', and the authors consider that this reflects the success of Irish industrial policy — which is, of course, closely related to Community regional policy. But the 'success' of industrial/regional policy has largely been in attracting foreign-owned firms producing relatively high technology products for export. For a number of reasons Ireland's success in this activity has not provided a basis for deeply-rooted industrialisation and, consequently, has not facilitated much convergence towards average EC national or regional income and unemployment levels.

For the reasons elaborated above, this failure to achieve real convergence cannot, on its own, support a definite judgement on Community structural policy — except, of course, the conclusion that the measures undertaken were not *sufficient* for cohesion. Other information and arguments are needed to allow us judge whether infrastructural investment, capital grants, and training (the main items funded since 1975) are *necessary* for achieving cohesion.

From the Treaty to the Policies

It is clear that there has been considerable development of both regional and social policy since the formation of the Community. Nevertheless, the original Treaty formulation, outlined in Section 2 (ii), can be seen to have shaped these policies, and the overall place of the cohesion question, in three important senses. First, Community social and, especially, regional policy were, and largely remain, national policies part-funded by the Community. Second, member states remained free to pursue regional and social policies which may cut across a Community cohesion objective. Third, although the objective of cohesion was, to some extent, a stated Community objective, its pursuit through national instruments meant that it was not taken into account in the main body of Community policies.

3. COHESION IN THE 1991 INTER GOVERNMENTAL CONFERENCES

(i) Sidelining the Cohesion Question

Despite the close connection between the cohesion issue and EMU in discussion and analysis of the Community system ever since the late 1960s, the issue figured to a relatively small extent in the 1991 Inter Governmental Conferences on political union and EMU. Indeed, it is remarkable that in explaining its Draft Treaty on EMU the Commission proposed that the cohesion question should not be considered at all in the conference on EMU.

This certainly signals a change in the place of the cohesion issue in the political discussion at the Community level. (Whether it implies a change in the position in real politics is a slightly different matter, discussed in Section 5, below). Two factors can explain the decoupling of EMU and the cohesion issue in recent years. Much the most significant is the tendency (or perhaps necessity) to pander to the concerns of the two member states perceived as reluctant about monetary union. Although German reluctance on EMU is not primarily due to anxiety about the Community budget, this factor, combined, until recently, with German scepticism about the role of structural interventions in solving income and unemployment problems, does seem to have made the Commission and some member states excessively cautious about raising the cohesion issue. Whatever about its ultimate success in stopping EMU, the British campaign on sovereignty would seem to have been hugely successful in undermining the Commission's willingness to talk about any aspect of EMU which has *fiscal* implications; the cohesion question is definitely in this category and has consequently been put to one side.

The second reason why cohesion has been decoupled from EMU is intellectual. The close connections between EMU and cohesion policies in the late 1960s and throughout the 1970s reflected an intellectual consensus and a body of economic doctrine some of which has since been undermined. In particular, there has been some loss of faith in the need for, and the effectiveness of, countercyclical macroeconomic policy and, more generally, greater scepticism about the ability of state interventions to improve economic performance. In Section 4, I ask whether it is analytically correct to decouple EMU from cohesion policies and whether debate at Community level adequately reflects the economic arguments.

(ii) Proposals before the Inter Governmental Conferences

Getting Cohesion on the Agenda

The Irish government described as "entirely unacceptable" the Commission's attempt to exclude the cohesion question from the conference on EMU. In this the Irish government certainly led the group of countries most concerned about the regional pattern of economic activity and income — Ireland, Spain, Portugal and Greece.

Despite their success in getting cohesion on the agenda, there remained sharp disagreement on whether the move to EMU necessitates a change in the place of the cohesion issue in the Treaty and the Community system. On the one side were a number of governments, led by the Irish and the Spanish, who argued that greater efficiency, equity and stability will be achieved if there is considerable enhancement of Community policies in fields which tend to reduce regional and social inequalities and cushion regions from adverse shocks. On the other side were a number of highly influential governments and, somewhat surprisingly, the Commission, who rejected the need for Treaty changes and insisted that, at most, the cohesion issue requires some increase in the existing Community policy — the Structural Funds. Some would resist even that.

The Irish Government's Proposals

This climate of opinion, and the emerging pattern at the IGC on political union, would seem to have conditioned the concrete proposals put forward by the Irish government.

In introducing its own proposals, the Irish government adopted an approach which linked concrete initiatives on cohesion to the ultimate structure of full economic and monetary union:

> Ireland considers that the final goal must be an integrated Community, with systems in place analogous to those in existing unions, which will ensure an equitable distribution of the resources of the union between all its regions. The Conference must give this goal the political support it requires and the Treaty provisions must be adequate to facilitate it.

It proposes Treaty changes mainly in Title V, on economic and social cohesion, and in Articles 2 and 3, which set out the basic aims and policies of the Community. It proposed that economic and social cohesion should be included as one of the Community's tasks in Article 2 and that to "the activities of the Community", listed in Article 3, should be added "the adoption of appropriate policies aimed at achieving economic and social cohesion".

In the Articles which deal specifically with cohesion, the Irish government proposed that Article 130a, which define cohesion and the reduction of regional disparities as Community objectives, should also require the Commission to submit a periodic report to the Council and the Parliament on progress in the attainment of these objectives. Where such progress is not satisfactory the Commission would be required to make proposals for appropriate Community and national measures to rectify the situation. Furthermore, the Council would decide, by qualified majority, on the appropriate Community measures.

It proposed that Article 130b be extended to say that the cohesion objective shall be taken into account, not only in the *implementation* of the common policies (as in the present Treaty) but also in the *formulation* of common policies, common activities and of EMU. Furthermore, in undertaking its periodic review the Commission would be required to report on "the manner in which the various means prescribed in Article 130b have contributed" to cohesion. Indeed, the Irish government proposed that Articles 130d and 130e require the Commission to "submit comprehensive proposals" on the action necessary to strengthen cohesion both during stage 2 and at the start of stage 3 of EMU.

Since the main element of the Irish proposal was the tri-annual Commission report on the cohesion question, this was a negotiating stance which did not look for strong new Treaty provisions on cohesion, but sought provisions which might provide leverage in future political negotiations. Indeed, an important aspect of Ireland's approach was its requirement that the necessary Treaty changes should be backed up by a political commitment by the Council and the Commission to early concrete measures to support cohesion, notably through a further strengthening of the Structural Funds. More generally, the approach is one which relies on future advocacy of the cohesion case within the politics of the Community and, in this sense, the current Treaty revision should be seen as part of a process, rather than a single event which fully determines future developments.

The Spanish Government's Proposals

The Spanish government submitted a substantial paper on cohesion to the IGC on political union (*Agence Europe*, 8 March, 1991). This paper began by looking at the cohesion question in the Community in historical perspective, from Article 2 of the Treaty of Rome through the Werner Report (1971), the MacDougall Report (1977), the Padoa-Schioppa Report (1987), to the Delors Report (1989) and the statement of the then President of the Bundesbank, Mr. Pohl, that monetary union required a fiscal compensation scheme. The Spanish paper contrasted this tradition of analysis and argument with the paucity of the current discussion of cohesion and it diagnosed the Community as suffering from "political amnesia".

It then identified some limits of the Community's present cohesion policies, which could, *pace* the Commission, be identified without waiting for the review of the Structural Fund due at the end of 1991. Specifically, the Community budget has not been adequately adapted to achieve cohesion and Article 130b (requiring the cohesion objective to be taken into account in common policies) has not been implemented. Furthermore, the Spanish government pointed out that EMU involves a significant move beyond 1992 and the Single Act and this implies the need for more developed machinery to increase cohesion.

The heart of the Spanish government's proposal was rejection of the assumption that "the objective of cohesion was fully covered by the use of the

Structural Funds" and assertion of the role of the Community budget in ensuring cohesion in EMU. The paper cited Padoa-Schioppa's diagnosis of the current weaknesses of the Community budget: its small size; its regressive revenue source and expenditure programmes; and the co-financing requirements of the Structural Funds. Turning to the future role for the budget the paper made a distinction between the *economic stabiliser,* proposed by the Commission, and the budgetary mechanisms which are necessary in EMU. It insisted that the budgetary mechanism proposed do not amount to a kind of "compensation" for moving to EMU; it is the economic stabiliser within Community economic policy which should be viewed as compensation for loss of the exchange rate instrument — since it is this which will replace that instrument and the balance of payments finance currently provided for by Article 108. Indeed, the Spanish paper made the point that it is entirely logical that the economic stabiliser or support mechanism be available to all countries that forego the exchange rate instrument.

Having made this distinction the paper argued that the budgetary mechanism is justified by considerations of efficiency, stability and equity in EMU. On this, the Spanish government's paper stated explicit agreement with the Irish government's argument that the final union must have a system of inter-state transfers analogous to those in existing federations. The Spanish paper purported to make concrete proposals for steps in that direction. It proposed an "embryonic mechanism" to be established now and envisaged that, as the Community develops, this would become the central instrument for cohesion. The immediate measures proposed include both reform of the Community's revenue raising methods, to make them less regressive, and, on the expenditure side, the establishment of a new financial instrument under Article 130b.[3] It is this which the Spanish envisage as "the instrument of cohesion *par excellence* in this last phase of integration (*Agence Europe,* 8 March, 1991).

The Spanish government argued that Article 130d should be revised along the lines suggested by Ireland, but with the explicit statement that the new inter-state compensation fund should support development of human and physical capital not currently covered by the Structural Funds. In other respects the Spanish paper supported the Irish government's argument for continuation and further development of the Structural Funds and implementation of Article 130b.

Turning to the implications of this paper for the Treaty we need only mention those which were additional to, or different from, the Irish government's proposals. The main difference was that the Spanish government proposed changes in Title II, Financial Provisions, which was not mentioned in the Irish government's submission. The Spanish government proposed to include in

[3]It is proposed that this new inter-state compensation fund be given a cohesion objective, that it be applied where income is less than 90 per cent of the Community average and that it be distributed according to population, surface area and relative prosperity. Article 130c should state that support from this fund would be conditional on national budgetary discipline as specified in the new Treaty.

Article 200 the provision that the "European Community should have a progressive system of own resources which covers all the expenses of the common policies". In addition, it proposed that a Declaration be attached to the Treaty stating that the Community should set its new multiannual financial framework before January, 1993. The Spanish proposed a new Article, 130d, stating that the Community's contribution to projects will be modulated as a function of the financial capacity of the member state in question.

Despite the citation of analytical arguments concerning the fiscal system of the Community and the mechanisms which are required in EMU, some of the logic and concrete proposals of the Spanish government are a little mysterious. The proposed new inter-state compensation fund, to be defined in the Treaty as a fund to support the development of human and physical capital, looks remarkably like more structural funds. To this extent the Spanish paper may not have been the most compelling application of the kind of analytical arguments presented in the NESC report *Ireland in the European Community* (NESC, 1989). Indeed, it is possible that the concrete proposals were designed more to address a Spanish grievance with the existing allocation of the Community budget than to put in place an 'embryonic mechanism' of fiscal federalism.

The Response to the Irish and Spanish Proposals

It is not possible to identify precisely the response to the Irish and Spanish proposals at the 1991 IGC. However, both the Commission's response and the subsequent Draft Treaty prepared by the Luxembourg Presidency have been published in *Agence Europe*.

The central element of the Commission's response was an acknowledgement of the need for some revision of Title V, on economic and social cohesion, but an insistence that cohesion must be seen first and foremost in terms of the effectiveness of Community structural policy. The Commission drew a sharp distinction between the question of amending *Treaty provisions* and the issue of *increased funding* for those policies. Furthermore, the Commission adhered to its original position that, pending the review of the structural policies which is due at the end of 1991, no major change could be made in the Treaty provisions or the principles governing these funds and policies. Indeed, it tended to draw attention to the fact that these policies are governed more by secondary legislation than by the Treaty.

The Irish government's proposals were reflected in some of the Treaty changes which the Commission then proposed. This was particularly so with respect to the idea of regular reviews to produce a balance sheet of progress towards cohesion. It should be noted, however, that the Irish proposal obliged the Commission to submit not only reviews of cohesion, but also comprehensive *proposals* for Community *action*. The Commission went somewhat beyond the Irish government's proposals in suggesting that the priority objectives of the structural policies, adopted in the Framework Regulation of 1988, could be written into the Treaty, and in indicating that the role of education policy and health policy in pursuing these objectives might be mentioned. The Commission also added to the Irish government's proposals by suggesting two interesting revisions of the decision-making process. It noted that the effectiveness of the structural policies could be improved by introducing qualified majority voting, instead of unanimity, into the Council's decisions on future Structural Fund regulations (Article 130d). It also suggested that the creation of new Structural Funds, or the amalgamation of existing ones, might be left to the legislative process rather than defined in the Treaty.

One senses that there was a much less positive Commission attitude to the Spanish government's paper and proposed Treaty changes. The Commission seemed intent on portraying the arguments raised in the Spanish paper as *purely political*. If this portrayal succeeded it would decouple the political *(sic)* case put forward in the Spanish paper from the economic analysis of the Padoa-Schioppa Report. It would also raise the genuine question of whether sufficient "political homogeneity" exists in the Community to achieve even an embryonic fiscal mechanism, and would, less genuinely, raise the spectre of the Spanish proposal re-opening a damaging budgetary squabble like the infamous British budgetary problem.

Cohesion in the New Treaty

It may be helpful to summarise the main change concerning cohesion in the new Treaty, as drafted by the Luxembourg Presidency in June, 1991. Economic and social cohesion is added to the objectives of the Community (as defined in Article 2) and, to the activities of the Community (listed in Article 3) is added "the strengthening of its economic and social cohesion". The most significant change is the addition to Article 130b of the requirement that "the Commission shall submit a report to the European Parliament and the Council every three years on the progress made towards achieving economic and social cohesion, accompanied if necessary by appropriate proposals". In addition, the Article refers to the possibility of actions 'outside the Funds'. Finally, Article 130d provides that the Council may regroup the existing Structural Funds or establish new ones.

In summary, Section 3 has surveyed the place of the cohesion question in the 1991 Inter Governmental Conferences. This has revealed an attempt to sideline the cohesion issue in political discussion in the Community in recent years. We traced this primarily to a tendency to assuage rather than confront fears about loss of sovereignty and growth in the Community budget. An additional factor has been a change in the intellectual climate. In studying the proposals on cohesion presented at the IGCs we considered the Irish government's proposals, the Spanish government's paper and Treaty suggestions, the Commission's apparent response and the new Treaty (as drafted by the Luxembourg Presidency mid-way through the conferences). Although there was considerable overlap between the Irish and Spanish proposals, there was some difference between the tactical approaches and concrete suggestions of the two governments.

4. THE REGIONAL PATTERN OF ECONOMIC ACTIVITY IN EMU

(i) Identifying the Issues

In deciding Ireland's attitude to the proposal for economic and monetary union a central issue is the likely regional distribution of economic activity and income in Europe. Will monetary union ease the problems of Irish firms and cause new firms to locate in Ireland? Or will it exacerbate existing difficulties and cause a further flow of capital and labour from Ireland to the more advanced, central, regions of Europe? Given that monetary union would be *permanent* these are clearly very important issues. It is equally clear that they are very large questions — depending as they do on long run tendencies in the world and European economies, the regional implications of technical and organisational change in modern firms, the economic effects of Ireland's social and political structures and values, and the effects of money on output, employment and inflation. Our knowledge on these issues is far from complete and usually the subject of sharp disagreement. It is clearly impractical to survey the state of knowledge on all these forces and, consequently, in this section I suggest a framework for analysis of the regional effects of EMU and identify some of the key arguments.

The method I adopt is to begin by stating a view of the regional implication of monetary union which dominated discussion of European monetary union for many years, and which is still of considerable significance, and then to ask whether, and in what way, this needs to be revised. The view in question is one which compares the possible regional effects of *monetary* union with the implications of lesser degrees of economic integration, such as a customs union and a common market, and *suggests that monetary union would impose significant short-run and long-run costs on weaker regions.* Consequently, in order to state and examine this proposition we need, first, to define these stages of integration.

Three Models of Economic Integration

Although integration is a complex process, which can vary in a large number of ways, three different levels of integration can be defined for the purposes of analysis.[4]

The Customs Union Model involves only the elimination of tariffs and quotas and adoption of a common external tariff.

The Common Market Model involves not only free trade but free movement of capital and labour. It also involves some common market-regulating policies, such as competition policy, which in turn implies that a small amount of revenue be raised for a Community budget.

---

[4]There are significant limitations to these textbook definitions and to the comparisons which can be made between them (see NESC, 1989, Chapter 13).

The Economic and Monetary Union Model (EMU) involves free trade, free movement of capital and labour, plus monetary integration (either a common currency or fixed exchange rates with close coordination of the states' macroeconomic policies). In addition, in an EMU many of the policies originally undertaken by the member states are now of concern at the Community level. This implies the existence of a much more substantial Community budget.

Outlining these definitions is useful, not only because it allows us to state and examine the textbook view about the costs of monetary union, but also because it makes clear what choice the voters face when they consider a new Treaty. The choice will not be between integration into the European, and world, economy, on the one hand, and independence or isolation on the other; instead, the choice will probably be between a common market, which involves free trade, freedom of capital movement and international labour mobility, on the one hand, and some form of economic and monetary union, on the other.

The Textbook View

The view of the regional implications of EMU which has dominated discussion of European monetary union, from the late sixties until very recently, is that it is the *monetary* stage of integration which presents weaker regions with the greatest problems. This view results from the following arguments. First, it was considered that the allocation of economic acitivity between member states would differ substantially depending on whether the states had formed a customs union, common market, or an EMU. The second important element of this viewpoint is that this difference was considered to have significant implications for the regional pattern of economic activity in a monetary union. In particular, it was argued that in weaker states and regions, which previously used exchange rate devaluation to support output and employment, adherence to a single monetary standard would be deflationary for significant periods.

It is because of these arguments that most discussion by economists of the regional implications of economic integration has focused on the *monetary* stage and, within that, has concentrated on the loss of exchange rate autonomy. It is also because of these arguments that a very large number of economists consider that monetary union should include a federal budgetary mechanism which would cushion regions from the worst effects of shocks in the way that exchange rate variation did before monetary union.[5] The procedure in this section is to explore the validity of this set of arguments.

An Alternative Perspective on EMU

I suggest an alternative perspective on the pattern and timing of the overall costs and benefits of integration for weaker regions. This involves, first and

[5]It is important to note that arguments for fiscal union do not depend on this view that adherence to a single monetary standard will be deflationary.

foremost a different view of the regional implications of *free trade* (the customs union stage) and *capital and labour mobility* (the common market stage). It suggests that even *free trade* can generate large and unevenly distributed costs and benefits in both the short and long run. Furthermore, it indicates that international movements of labour and capital may widen rather than narrow the differences between regional economies. At the very least, this alternative perspective takes the emphasis off *monetary* union as the step which raises problems for weaker economies. The second step in the evaluation of the textbook view is to then assess the specifically *monetary* argument concerning the macroeconomic effects of the loss of exchange rate autonomy. A third step is to extend the analysis of the monetary element beyond issues of *macroeconomic* management to a consideration of the implication of monetary union for financial flows and the availability of finance in different regions of a single monetary and financial zone. This line of argument suggests that, as a first approximation, we can consider the *economic* forces, unleashed by free trade and mobility of labour and capital, as separate from the monetary factors. In (ii), below, I elaborate in a little more detail the economic tendencies to regional convergence and divergence and, in (iii), consider some regional aspects of the monetary factor.

(ii) Regional Tendencies in an Economic Union

This section presents, in summary fashion, arguments concerning tendencies for regional convergence and divergence which can be found in regional economics and the economics of international trade.[6] It is on the basis of these that we question two important elements of the textbook view outlined above — first, that, unlike monetary integration, the effects of free trade and factor mobility are fairly benign and, second, that the international pattern of economic activity will be very different depending on whether Ireland is in a customs union, a common market or an EMU.

Regional Convergence by Market Forces

Mainstream economic theory, based on the notion of the economy as a self-adjusting mechanism, formulates the regional dimension in a way which stresses the tendency to regional balance. According to this theory, the normal functioning of supply and demand will tend to achieve full utilisation of all resources within each region and, more significantly in the current context, tend to eliminate disparities between different regions. This theory of regional convergence is widely considered to be invalid since it is based on some highly unrealistic assumptions. The implication of this is, as Padoa-Schioppa says, that

[6]These arguments are spelled out in more detail in the NESC report *Ireland in the European Community* (NESC, 1989).

"any easy extrapolation of 'invisible hand' ideas to the real world of regional economics in the presence of market-opening measures would be unwarranted in the light of economic history and theory" (Padoa-Schioppa, 1987).

Forces Making for Regional Concentration of Economic Activity

A much more promising approach to understanding the existence and persistence of regional inequalities is that which invokes the 'principle of cumulative causation'. If there are 'economies of scale in production' (the cost of production of goods fall as output increases) or if there are 'economies of agglomeration' (the cost of production is lower because of the proximity of other firms) then a region which gets an initial advantage will find that advantage reinforced as its level of production increases. Each time output is increased, costs fall and other regions find it more difficult to catch up. If the strong region attracts capital and labour from weaker regions, this will further enhance its productive potential and, because of the economies of scale and of agglomeration, strengthen its competitive advantage. Hence the label 'cumulative causation': output growth, by lowering costs, developing skills and know-how, inducing innovation and specialisation creates a self-sustaining growth process in certain regions; but other regions may find themselves in a cycle of decline. In this view, economic disparities, far from being self-adjusting or self-correcting, as in the orthodox vision, tend to be *self-reinforcing*.

The existence and importance of economies of agglomeration is related to one of the most fundamental processes of economic development — the division of labour. As the division of labour develops, inter-firm transactions become numerous and complex: flows of materials, subcontracting relations, face-to-face exchanges of information, and so on. This creates strong pressures for geographical concentration of industry. In recent work on the regional distribution of economic activity access to these information networks is given even more emphasis than economies of scale in production. These ideas have been used to explain the development of the Lancashire cotton complex of the nineteenth century, the semi-conductor industry in Silicon Valley, California, in the 1960s and 1970s, and Route 128 in Massachusetts in the 1980s (Scott and Storper, 1986).

Other factors which reinforce the tendency to concentration are advantageous labour market characteristics (enhanced by migration from poorer regions) and economies of scale in the provision of infrastructure.

Yet another recently studied advantage of concentration is *innovation leadership*. Empirical work has revealed evidence of remarkable concentration both of industrial research activity by private and public sector organisations, and of actual manufacturing innovations in core regions. A recent OECD Report, *Structural Adjustment and Economic Performance* highlights the significance of manufacturing expertise as a prerequisite for reaping the benefits of innovation. It notes that such expertise "grows by cumulative effects of learning, scale and sector cross-fertilisation" and, is "contrary to the assumptions of the orthodox theory of comparative advantage . . . geographically concentrated" (OECD, 1987, p. 256). Firms and countries that have acquired this manufacturing know-how are well placed to take an even larger share of the value-added made possible by technical progress.

In a recent theoretical paper, entitled 'Increasing Returns and Economic Geography', Krugman concludes that the tendency for industry to concentrate in the large "central" economies depend on three factors: *economies of scale, transport costs and the size of the manufacturing sector.*

> If transportation costs are high, return to scale weak, and the share of spending on manufactured goods low, the incentive to produce close to the market leads to an equal division of manufacturing between the regions. With lower transport costs, stronger scale economies, or a higher manufacturing share, circular causation sets in: the more manufacturing is located in one region, the larger that region's share of demand, and this provides an incentive to locate still more manufacturing there.

Furthermore, this analysis suggests that the economic history of regions can be influenced by the conditions prevailing at critical moments — a slight population or other advantage can lead to lasting dominance, but "had the distribution of population at that critical moment been only slightly different, the roles of the regions might have been reversed" (Krugman, 1989, p. 7).

This formidable list of arguments would seem to justify the interim conclusion that there are considerable forces making for concentration of advanced economic activity. If this is what emerges from *regional economics* it is of interest to ask how consistent it is with what is found in the *economics of international trade* and economic integration.

The New Economics of International Trade

One reason why the textbook theory of economic integration viewed monetary integration as more likely to exacerbate regional problems was that the relative costs and benefits of a customs union, a common market and an economic and monetary union were assessed by applying the traditional theory of international trade. That traditional theory was based on very restrictive assumptions and these had a major role in generating the benign view of trade in the conventional literature. In recent years significant developments have occurred in the theory of international trade and integration. The new approach takes account of important real world phenomena such as economies of scale, external economies, the market power of firms and learning by doing. The important point is that these new approaches alter somewhat our views of the gains from trade and integration (see NESC, 1989).

Limitations of space preclude a detailed discussion of how these new trade theories alter our views of the gains from trade. However, for a reason that will emerge presently, the issue is an important one and a brief summary is warranted.

In general, the new approaches to trade indicate that the overall gains from trade and integration are potentially larger than in the conventional analysis. In addition, the new theories provide some reasons to believe that the costs of adjusting to free trade will be more evenly distributed between regions, and some reasons why the long run benefits of trade will be *less evenly* distributed — depending, to a large extent on the initial economic structures of the countries and regions entering into integration. Krugman summarises this difference by saying that trade based on economies of scale, the market power of firms and product differentiation "probably involves less conflict of interest within countries and more conflict between countries than conventional trade" (Krugman, 1987).[7]

Thus the general view of uneven regional development outlined above is one which finds a clear echo in the theory of international trade. Furthermore, this view is also found in the vast majority of studies which consider the regional distribution of the benefits of European market *integration.* To cite but two examples, Padoa-Schioppa, in his important study of the Community system, considers that "the spatial distribution of such gains is less certain and is unlikely to be even" (1987). Finally, and specifically on the completion of the single market, Pelkmans and Robson say that the structural problems of the less advanced member states "will almost certainly be accentuated by an approach to fully-fledged industrial market integration" (1987).

Two Important Qualifications

The existence of a strong tendency to regional concentration of advanced economic activity should not be understood as implying that industry will definitely concentrate and regional fortunes will definitely diverge. The process of regional development and change is not as deterministic as some accounts of 'cumulative causation' suggest. This is so for two distinct reasons. First, it would be very surprising if there were not also counter tendencies. Below, we identify some forces making for *diffusion* of activity, especially manufacturing. Second, the process of regional change, just like the process of economic development, is not a steady journey along a path of either concentration or dispersal. It is an inherently uneven process which progresses in bursts of

[7]This statement is explained in a non-technical way in NESC, 1989, Chapter 2.

progress and sharp reversals. This unpredictability and contingency suggests that other forces — not included in the lists of those which create underlying tendencies to concentration and dispersal — are also very important and, furthermore, that among these might be such factors as political and social structures and economic policies. This unpredictability and contingency is reflected in the more interesting recent research in regional economics, the economics of trade and integration and development economics.

In regional economics it is recognised that although there are tendencies to concentration (and, to a lesser extent, tendencies to dispersal) there is, in fact, a *shifting hierarchy* of leading and lagging regions. Although analysis of these shifts is at a very rudimentary level this line of enquiry suggests that a region's fortunes are not fully determined by external or immutable forces making for concentration. Furthermore, it is recognised that factors indigenous to a region or country can influence the role which it assumes in the international division of labour.

In the new approach to international trade this non-deterministic outlook is reflected in the fact that simple economies of scale in production and market size are not the only factors influencing the pattern of trade and production and the relative gains from trade. Indeed, it is recognised that one of the most important sources of economies of scale and the market power of firms, lies in the dynamic process by which firms and industries improve their technologies. This emphasis on innovation suggests the significance of firms' strategies, but also of the institutional factors which support or inhibit innovation. In addition, the emphasis on strategic sectors, which emerges in the new analysis of trade, strongly suggests an important determining role for policy within a state or region.

Forces for Diffusion of Manufacturing Industry

It is clear that since World War II, large corporations have chosen to locate different parts of their businesses in very different regions and countries. In particular, manufacturing plants have frequently been located in less developed and peripheral areas. In addition, many of the traditional industrial regions in advanced countries seem to have become 'de-industrialised'.

To this pressure for diffusion of certain industrial activities may be added the effect of improvements in transport and telecommunications infrastructure which can, in certain circumstances, reduce the economic significance of distance. Another factor limiting regional imbalances is the fact that rapid growth in central areas puts a strain on their infrastructure and creates congestion costs.

Do these arguments warrant the conclusion that the forces of diffusion are such that the completion of the single market may be expected to coincide with a narrowing of the disparities between rich and poor regions in Europe? In my judgement the answer must be: no. There are two reasons for reaching this conclusion. First, the diffusion of industry as a result of the 'new spatial division of labour' is not the only force influencing the pattern of regional development; some of the other forces at work, such as technical and organisational changes, tend to maintain or even reinforce concentration. Second, even where the new spatial division of labour is creating a diffusion of certain manufacturing activities, this diffusion is not likely to bring about convergence of regional incomes and economic structures (see NESC, 1989, pp. 321–27).

(iii) Regional Aspects of the Monetary Union

The traditional emphasis on the monetary step as the stage of integration which generates problems for weaker regions, was based on a particular reading of free trade and mobility of capital and labour, combined with a pessimistic view of the loss of exchange rate autonomy. Recent work questions the benign view of the regional distribution of gains from free trade and factor mobility and this has, at the very least, taken the emphasis off monetary integration as the only step which raises problems for weaker regions. We must now consider the monetary question itself.

The main question concerns the effects of permanently foregoing the option of exchange rate devaluation or revaluation. Most discussions of the monetary issue are confined to this macroeconomic question. In our view there is another dimension which requires consideration. Will formation of a monetary union, and a single financial area, alter the regional flows of savings and loans and thereby constrain the regional pattern of liquidity and availability of finance? This issue is discussed in Patrick Honohan's *Monetary Union*, the previous paper in this book.

Monetary Union and the Loss of Exchange Rate Autonomy

The pessimistic view of the regional implications of monetary union has two components. First, if weaker regions have a worse underlying trade-off between inflation and unemployment, then imposing the same inflation rate on all regions, which is one effect of monetary union, will imply higher unemployment in weaker regions (Corden, 1972). Second, when economic fluctuations occur which affect some regions more than others, commonly referred to as 'asymmetric shocks', the impossibility of exchange rate devaluation means that output, employment and unemployment in the unlucky region will bear the full brunt of the shock. For a reason that will emerge presently, these two propositions should be kept distinct from one another.

The monetarist revolution has severely challenged the analytical foundations of this traditional view. Put most simply, monetarist theory says that devaluation offers no protection to output and employment, but simply changes prices in the country devaluing. This alone suggests that the loss of the exchange rate instrument is no loss.

While many economists are now persuaded that devaluation has limited ability to defend employment, in the case of many monetarists, this idea is linked to a much more general proposition about the determination of output and employment, and the relationship between money supply and the level of real activity in the economy. That general proposition is that the real economy in each country (or in a monetary union) has a natural tendency to *full* employment and, consequently, it would be logically impossible for a change in the exchange rate, or any other macroeconomic policy, to increase output and employment further. In short, this theory says that there is no trade-off between inflation and unemployment, in either strong or weak regions, and hence disposes of the first component of the pessimistic view of monetary union. Carried to its logical conclusion this theory also dismisses the second component of that view: it suggests that wages and prices will adjust to rapidly restore full employment after an asymmetric shock — a performance that could not be improved upon by exchange rate devaluation.

What are we to make of this wholesale dismissal of all traditional anxieties about the effect of monetary union on unemployment? Three points allow us gain a perspective on the issue.

First, experience does indeed suggest that devaluation is a less powerful instrument than was once assumed. Rather than make a very general statement (see below) it may be sufficient to say that, in the circumstances prevailing in Ireland (a small economy with a very high propensity to import), exchange rate devaluation offers policy makers a very limited instrument for increasing output and employment and makes it more difficult to achieve low inflation.

But, second, the evidence does not support the view, which is suggested by some, that the exchange rate is *completely powerless* to influence competitiveness, output or employment. The authors of *One Market, One Money* say that "nominal exchange rates may have an impact on real exchange rates for, say, two to five years, but this does not persist in the long run" (Commission, 1990b, p. 140). Indeed, the strong theoretical position against the significance of the exchange rate is undermined by the historical evidence of successful devaluations and, more emphatically, disastrous overvaluations. This does not make the case for devaluation but it disposes of an absolute, theoretically-based, rejection of the idea. When assesssing the merits of devaluation other considerations arise which suggest that it could only be successfully used *infrequently* — but that, in certain crisis situations, it could provide a breathing space, either to ride out a temporary crisis or to undertake adjustment to a permanent shift in economic conditions.

Third, regardless of the effectiveness or ineffectiveness of devaluation at the current stage of integration, in EMU there are likely to be problems which affect different regions differently, and which therefore generate regional macro-economic imbalances. These problems will be no more likely to solve themselves rapidly and painlessly, by means of price and wage adjustment, than they are now. Consequently, it has frequently been argued that a European monetary union would work more effectively if it were also a fiscal union. The raising of union revenue, and its expenditure on a range of Community policies, would provide an element of automatic adjusting mechanism which would tend to cushion regions from the worst effects of asymmetric shocks (Eichengreen, 1990). This position, though widely accepted by economists, is flatly contracted in the Commission's recent report *One Market, One Money*.

General Principles for a Currency Area: Size and Social Unity

Perhaps the most general analysis of the relative merits of currency independence and monetary union is that of Goodhart, of the London School of Economics and previously an adviser at the Bank of England. He attempts to reduce various analytical approaches to a few general principles:

> There appear to be two common factors here determining whether the balance-of-payments adjustments of some geographical area would be more easily solved as a region within a common-currency area or as an independent country with a separate and a potentially-variable exchange rate. These are size, and social unity with surrounding, contiguous regions (Goodhart, 1989, p. 420).

The smaller the size of the region the easier it will adjust within a common currency area and the harder it will find it to run an effective independent monetary and exchange rate policy. In Goodhart's judgement the more important factor is social unity. The reason is that if this exists then fiscal mechanisms will be in place which will ease and even possibly solve regional disparities. He considers that an attempt to impose an exchange-rate union without the support of a strong, centralised, or at least inter-regionally coordinated, fiscal policy could have serious regional effects.

In discussing this subject Goodhart puts his finger on a problem which we identify below as very relevant to the current position of the cohesion issue in the Community system. This is what he refers to as a chicken and egg problem:

> I have argued both that a single-currency area requires a strong, centralised fiscal authority, ready and able to ease regional adjustment problems, and also that it will be difficult to establish any effective centralised fiscal authority covering areas with independent, separate currencies (Goodhart, 1989, p. 424).

While he does not offer any practical way out of this chicken and egg problem, the close connection which he sees between monetary union and social unity, and also between control of currency and national sovereignty, lead him to say emphatically that: "Fiscal and monetary harmonisation will march together, or not at all". One of the main conclusions of my argument is that political union and cohesion will march together, or not at all (see Section 5, below). But, given my view of what is required for cohesion, this amounts to a very similar position to that of Goodhart.

5. ISSUES FOR IRELAND AND THE COMMUNITY

(i) Overview of the Issues

The discussion of issues for Ireland and the Community should begin by considering whether cohesion considerations suggest that Ireland should support or oppose EMU. However, it is readily shown that cohesion considerations provide no compelling general argument against EMU, and that, on certain conditions, cohesion is more likely to be achieved in an advanced stage of economic, monetary and political integration than in the current situation. It follows that the question of deciding for or against EMU constitutes only a small part of the discussion of the issues thrown up by the earlier analysis of cohesion.

Once the decision in favour of EMU in principle has been made, the next problem is to identify how to achieve cohesion. I begin by emphasising the importance of domestic policy. The discussion of the regional tendencies in an economic union, in Section 4, above, indicated that factors indigenous to a region, including economic and other policies, can have a significant effect on its performance in an open international economy. In addition, strong domestic policies can have an influence on the discussion at Community level and on the willingness of the Community to develop its own policies. Next, I briefly survey four areas of Community policy which can contribute to cohesion and assess the potential and limitations of each. This indicates that the greatest Community contribution to cohesion is likely to arise from the development of the Community budget which would occur when the scope of Community policy widens and monetary union is accompanied by an element of fiscal union. It is important to identify the conditions in which this development would occur and to see that among these is a condition known as political homogeneity or political cohesion. This has implications for Ireland's approach to Community matters across a wide range of policy areas.

In the light of these arguments it is possible to consider the various approaches to the cohesion issue at the 1991 Inter Governmental Conferences and in the current process of construction of EMU. It is argued that despite the recent tendency to sever the traditional connection between the EMU project and cohesion policies, there remains analytical reasons to consider the two together.

Irish discussion of the IGCs and the new Treaty will inevitably tend to focus on the cohesion issue and the somewhat different approach of the Irish and Spanish governments. There are a number of considerations which should inform any such discussion. This is important because an initial comparison might suggest that the Spanish argument is more closely, or at least more wholeheartedly, based on the main analytical ideas sketched above (concerning the links between economic, monetary and fiscal integration). In another sense, however, the Irish government's approach can be seen to be consistent with that analysis: the very limits of the ambition of the current revision of the Treaty suggests that the degree of political homogeneity or political cohesion is not about to be greatly increased and, on the analysis of this paper, this limits the progress which can be made on economic and social cohesion. The real issue about the Irish government's attitude in the current negotiations is whether its overall approach, across the range of political and economic issues, has been such as to encourage and facilitate a deepening of the political cohesion upon which economic cohesion ultimately depends.

The paper finishes by briefly noting some issues for the future which need to be considered if real progress on cohesion is to made. Among these is the relationship between regional and social inequality and, therefore, the meaning of cohesion. The power of regional, or spatial, policies to solve, what are seen as regional problems is dependent on an understanding of the factors which cause those problems. In this context, there is a need for serious work on the true nature and relevance of peripherality. It cannot be taken for granted that Ireland's competitive disadvantage arises because of *distance*.

(ii) Deciding on Monetary Union

Ireland's attitude to EMU must be formed by assessing it on three criteria. The first is the likely regional pattern of economic activity and income in a European EMU. The second is the implications of EMU for the microeconomic performance or efficiency of the Irish economy. The third criterion is whether the macroeconomic performance of Ireland and Europe is likely to be superior, and macroeconomic management more successful, in EMU than at present. The concern in this paper has been with the first of these, and the latter two are mentioned only briefly.

Regional Patterns at Different Stages of Integration

The approach to this issue has been to re-examine an influential view that it is the step to monetary integration which can give rise to problems for weaker regions. I have questioned this view in two ways. First, it has been shown that the relatively negative attitude to monetary union which it suggests, derives, in part, from the extremely positive view of earlier stages of economic integration, such as free trade and mobility of capital and labour. That benign view of the regional effects of trade and factor mobility arises from the application of the traditional theory of international trade. Application of the more realistic, new, analysis of trade and factor mobility suggests that these stages of integration can generate large and unevenly distributed costs and benefits in both the short and long run.

The second element of the influential traditional view which has been questioned is the idea that the loss of the exchange rate instrument would greatly increase the exposure of a small country like Ireland to crises of unemployment. While some reject that idea on the grounds that such crises are not likely to occur, or are less likely to occur in EMU, this has not been the approach here. The argument is simply that, in Ireland's circumstances, autonomous exchange rate policy offers a very limited power to ameliorate the effects of economic fluctuations and complicates the pursuit of anti-inflation policy.

The effect of this re-examination is, at the very least, to take the emphasis off monetary union as the stage of integration which is likely to give rise to problems for weaker regions.

In deciding whether to advance to monetary union we have to consider both the regional pattern of activity, as determined by market forces, and the regional effects of public policy. Before commenting on the latter it may be useful to summarise my view of the regional effects of market forces. The main argument is that the major determinants of regional development are probably real ones, rather than monetary factors. This focus on the economic forces suggests that there are a number of reasons why the effect of market forces in shaping the pattern of activity across member states may not, in fact, be very different at different stages of integration. The underlying determinants of regional development (technology, market size, innovation, resources, internal economic organisation etc.) will make themselves felt so long as a region or country is in any way integrated into the international system. Many of the most important forces making for regional convergence and divergence are inseparable from the internationalisation of economic activity which exists independently of the fact that countries embark on formal integration. Consequently, many of those forces are likely to be influencing Ireland regardless of whether we are in a customs union, a common market, or an economic and monetary union.

The Regional Effects of Public Policy

The regional pattern of activity and income in Europe will be determined not only by market forces but also by public policy. What can we say of the regional effects of public policy in EMU as compared with present arrangements? There are three dimensions of public policy that are relevant: Community policy, other member states' policy and domestic policy.

When we consider the potential regional effects of Community policy in EMU we face a problem which was highlighted in Section 1. The scope and content of Community policy is not completely determined by reference to technical definitions of a common market or EMU but are, in fact, contested by different interest groups.

The range of Community policy will depend on the 'economic order' which prevails in Europe and this will be determined largely by political and economic competition. This is not to say that rational arguments and analytical principles can have no role in determining the scope and content of Community policy. Indeed, there are a strong set of analytical principles which imply that a successful economic and monetary union would require that the Community tier be involved in a wide range of policy functions and that, for this and other reasons, the Community would have significant elements of fiscal union. In addition, there is a compelling case that the resulting set of fiscal mechanisms can play an important role in cushioning regions of the union from the worst effects of asymmetric shocks — in the same way that exchange rate movements were intended to do. This would suggest that the full range of Community policies (microeconomic, macroeconomic and distributive) would be likely to produce a more favourable regional pattern in advanced EMU than in lesser stages of integration, such as we are in at the present.

The problem is, of course, that national political considerations of governments, reflecting the weakness of political cohesion, have meant that these analytical arguments have frequently been ignored. As a result, the Community has a limited range of common policies and even its control of these is continually hampered by national governments. In addition, the Community has a minute and regressive fiscal system which accords with no rational principles of public finance. Does this suggest that in assessing the likely regional impact of Community policy in EMU we should forget the analytical arguments and expect very little by way of fiscal union?

While that outlook cannot be dismissed out of hand, it may be based on an overly static view of the Community. National governments' attempts to hinder the development and implementation of common policies, however firmly based on preceived national attitudes, are never sufficient to make the underlying issues go away entirely. For example, having abolished tariffs, the states proceeded to negate the common market with new non-tariff barriers; but eventually the logic of the international economy, and of their own decision to integrate, could be ignored no longer. No doubt, further functional and logical implications of the single market will now be evaded for a period, because they are seen to encroach on the prerogatives of national interests and states. But, sooner or later, they too will be faced up to. There is no reason to believe that EMU should be any different. While the new Treaty which will almost certainly duck many of the issues of EMU, especially those deriving from the analytical principles mentioned above, there will follow a dynamic economic and political process which will create opportunities to bring the issues to light.

When we consider the regional effects of other member states' policies we find that these are very likely to be more favourable to social and spatial cohesion in EMU than at present. One concrete change of relevance to Ireland would be an end to gyrations of sterling. But the main point is not specifically related to monetary union. Deeper economic union, and especially an enforcement of competition policy, would constrain national policies which support regions and firms and tend to negate Community regional policy.

Finally, we must consider the regional effects of *domestic* policy in EMU, compared with present arrangements. This would once have been discussed mainly in terms of the loss of exchange rate autonomy and the consequent possibility of region-specific crises. While the loss of exchange rate autonomy should now be viewed as less significant, the overall effect of economic integration on domestic policy is now understood to be much greater than was once believed. Section 1 explained that the integration of mixed economies "drastically undermine(s) the delicately balanced packages of public policy regulation, market intervention, income redistribution measures and macroeconomic policies that are at present determined at the level of national politics" (Pelkmans and Robson, 1987). This applies to monetary union, not only because it removes the exchange rate instrument, but also because it considerably deepens the general integration of markets and, specifically, because it constrains national fiscal policy. The implications of economic and monetary integration for national fiscal systems was a central theme of NESC's report, *Ireland in the European Community*. The constraint on domestic fiscal policy will arise, in part, from the legal control which the Community will exercise over national budget deficits. However, this is likely to be the least significant aspect of the constraint on fiscal policy. In their analysis of Ireland's position in the Community, NESC concluded that not only will indirect taxes be harmonised by Community law, in order to remove customs frontiers, but deeper market integration "will greatly increase the existing pressure for approximation of income and some other direct taxes in the Community, if tax-induced migration of labour and capital are to be minimised" (NESC, 1989, p. 383). It follows that economic and monetary union will impose constraints on both the structure and rates of taxation and on total revenue raised by national authorities — a point which is recognised by the Commission in its major statement on EMU of 21 August 1990 (Commission, 1990c, p. 23). Indeed, this is one of the reasons why the link between EMU and cohesion policies remains analytically valid (see (iii), below).

It should not be inferred that these constraints on domestic policy will be uniformly or unambiguously harmful to cohesion. Indeed, NESC pointed out that some of the changes in taxation which the single market and monetary union will "force" on Ireland are highly desirable in their own right (NESC, 1989). But, as NESC puts it:

> . . . since the public expenditure requirements of member states are not uniform, pressure towards uniformity of several major sources of tax revenue could force some member states into budgetary imbalance or into inappropriate cuts in public expenditure. For example, the pressure to equalise major revenue raising taxes — which NESC accepts as an unavoidable concomitant of integration — could frustrate the pursuit of adjustment or regional policy objectives (NESC, 1989, p. 385).

In addition to these constraints on taxation, economic and monetary union will impose some constraints on the content of domestic policies.

These arguments imply that we can definitely say that domestic policy will be more constrained in EMU, but we cannot say that the regional effects of such policy will be uniformly less favourable than at present. The constraints on the structure and size of domestic revenue, and expenditure (given Community control of deficits), is likely to be the major factor. This brings us back once again to the scope and content of Community policy. The general implication of the new insight into the economic integration of mixed economies is that this requires not only the removal of barriers (negative integration) but also establishment of Community policies and institutions in a wide range of areas (positive integration). This applies to most economic policies and, given the regional effects of many policies (particularly taxation and public expenditure), it encompasses the cohesion issue.

Microeconomic Efficiency and Macroeconomic Performance

This discussion has concentrated on only one of the three criteria upon which a decision for or against EMU must be made. This has suggested that cohesion considerations provide no compelling general case against EMU — though the implications for cohesion will depend, in part, on the political evolution of the Community. It is not possible to discuss here the two remaining criteria, microeconomic efficiency and macroeconomic performance. However, it can be said that on these two criteria EMU seems, on balance, positive for Ireland. The reason for this is explained in the other sections in this book.

(iii) Policy Approaches to Cohesion

Introduction

Once the decision in favour of EMU has been made, the question of cohesion becomes the more practical one of devising ways to promote Ireland's progress towards average Community living standards and levels of unemployment. It is important to stress the role of domestic policy. Consideration is then given to the range of Community policies which could assist cohesion and briefly assess the potential and limits of each. This turns out to have an important political implication for Ireland.

The Importance of Domestic Policy

The analysis reported in Section 4 suggest that there are considerable forces making for geographic concentration of advanced economic activity. However, in reporting this idea it was emphasised that the existence of a tendency to concentration does not imply that this is an *inevitable* outcome and that the economic fortunes of the centre and the periphery must diverge. There would seem to be a shifting hierarchy of leading and lagging regions. Most importantly, there is definite evidence that factors indigenous to a region have a significant bearing on its performance and even on the place which it occupies in the international division of labour. Furthermore, among these indigenous factors are the economic and other policies pursued by national or regional authorities. This suggests that the first requirement for cohesion is domestic policies which promote the long-term strength of the Irish economy.

NESC placed great emphasis on this point. From its detailed analysis of Ireland's experience in the Community, it derived, and stated bluntly, a series of lessons. Of twelve lessons of the period 1973 to 1987, half refer to Irish policy rather than to international integration *per se*. This reflects NESC's finding that the effects of integration were conditioned by domestic policy. Indeed, it has subsequently been argued that "recognition of this interaction between economic integration, domestic policy and initial structural characteristics is central to a balanced assessment of Community membership" (Keatinge, *et al.*, 1991). These considerations led NESC to the view "that membership of the Community does not diminish the need for a national ability to identify solutions to national problems — even where these solutions require Community policies and action" (NESC, 1989, p. 218).

Domestic policy is vital not only because it influences the structure and performance of the Irish economy, but also because it constitutes an input at Community level. NESC stressed that the point about domestic policy "is valid in all contingencies":

> A firm national grasp of how to solve a problem strengthens the argument for adoption of a common or Community policy. It helps enormously when agreement to adopt a common approach is achieved. In the case where a Community policy is not achieved, a member state is on its own, and must have well-worked-out solutions to its problems — or fail to solve them (NESC, 1989, p. 218).

This is true across a wide range of policies, but is nowhere more important than in policies designed to reduce regional and social disparities. It constitutes a major challenge to Irish policy makers.

Community Policies which Influence Cohesion

We can identify at least four types of Community policy which influence regional and social disparities:

- structural policies
- macroeconomic coordination

– budgetary or fiscal mechanisms

– differential application of other Community policies.

It is important that both member states and the Community take a broad and realistic view of what can be, and what is likely to be, achieved by each of these types of policies in the pursuit of economic and social cohesion. It is not possible to undertake a detailed analysis of the potential and limits of these four approaches. However, the two main points which emerge from such an analysis should be reported, since they have implications for policy in moving towards EMU.

First, a study of regional problems and policies, and the evidence on Community regional policy assembled in Section 2, above, strongly suggest that the Structural Funds will not be sufficient to achieve cohesion in the Community. It is most important to realise that this is so not only because of the limited size of the Structural Funds, but also because knowledge of the nature and processes of regional development has not yet reached the stage where plans capable of really reversing regional decline, or initiating regional growth, are available to member states or the Commission. Indeed, regional development policy internationally has changed significantly in recent years and it remains to be seen whether new approaches (focusing on innovation, training, indigenous firms and service industries) are effective. These conclusions suggest that a major task facing Ireland and the Community is to develop the knowledge on which to build more effective regional development plans.

Second, the greatest Community contribution to cohesion is likely to arise from the development of the Community budget. While the most regressive, and therefore anti-cohesion, features of the Community budget could be removed immediately, the major promotion of cohesion will occur when the Community budget increases in line with the growing Community involvement in policy areas with European-wide effects. Indeed, in existing federations the federal budgetary mechanism makes a much more significant contribution to the reduction of regional disparities than structural policies do. This was widely recognised and much discussed in the main reports on EMU during the 1960s and 1970s.

It is important to appreciate that the argument for a greater degree of fiscal union in the Community is not one that is based solely, or even primarily, on considerations of regional *equity* or *redistribution*. The essential argument has a large efficiency dimension: that achievement of a genuine common market, and of efficiency within it, requires Community involvement in a wide range of policy areas. Thus the Community budget and greater fiscal union would grow as a concomitant of the growth of the Community's competence in various policy fields (see NESC, 1989, Chapter 13). In its main statement on EMU, of 21 August 1990, the Commission makes a similar point to that made here, and explored in detail by NESC:

> For improving economic efficiency a growing Community involvement in policy areas with European-wide effects should be foreseen and, when necessary, present Treaty provisions be extended or modified . . . Community finance should reflect and support the gradually increasing Community contribution to the attainment of the principal economic policy objectives related to efficiency, cooperation and economic and social cohesion (Commission, 1990c, p. 26).

The analytical arguments for Community involvement in a wider range of policies and for the development of a fiscal union have been presented elsewhere, and this explains the focus on the cohesion dimension of the budgetary issue in this section. However, one strand of the public finance argument does need to be briefly mentioned here.

Political Homogeneity: A Condition for Development of Community Policy

In the analytical approach to the assignment of policy areas to the various tiers of government in a federal (or unitary) system, one necessary condition for the allocation of a given policy to the highest, or Community, tier is what is known as "political homogeneity". The MacDougall group, in their famous Report *The Role of Public Finance in European Integration* (1977), defined this as follows:

> By political homogeneity is meant the degree of cohesion between member states that would enable a function to be dealt with at the Community level if *other reasons* existed for doing this (MacDougall, 1977, emphasis added).

At any point in time, the degree of political homogeneity is a matter of fact, defined by Community legitimacy under the Treaties and by current practice. But, over longer periods, it is something which changes and develops. Indeed, ultimately it relates to the choice of constitution for the Community — the very thing done at the current 1991 IGCs. Using this analytical approach to the question of Community public finance, the Irish social partners recently highlighted the connection between political homogeneity and cohesion:

> This has significant implications for a country which perceives its goals as most likely to be achieved in an economic union with a developed Community budget. Its strategic and tactical approach should be oriented to creating that 'degree of cohesion between member states' which would enable functions to be dealt with at the Community level, where there are already strong reasons for doing this. Furthermore, so long as the economic analysis of public finance, of the sort used by MacDougall and in this report, is brought to bear on these matters, it will not be realistic to see cohesion, as Irish governments seem to have, as a *purely economic* phenomenon which can be achieved prior to, or independently of, 'political homogeneity'. This is because the lack of sufficient 'political homogeneity' or 'degree of cohesion

between member states' may then be cited as a reason *not to* allocate a given function to the Community; and yet the formation of a Community policy may be necessary for the achievement of 'cohesion', defined in its narrowly economic sense (NESC, 1989, p. 422).

This reinforces the view that what is needed is a strategic approach to European integration and not separate tactical approaches to policy area such as the single market, monetary union, CAP reform, cohesion, institutional balance, foreign policy, security and defence.

(iv) Policy Approaches to Cohesion at the Inter Governmental Conferences

Reasserting the Analytical Links Between EMU and Cohesion

We saw in Section 2 (iii), that in discussion of monetary union since the late 1960s, EMU was closely linked with the cohesion issues and particularly with regional problems and policies. It was shown in Section 3, that in very recent years this connection has been weakened — to such an extent that the Commission could seriously suggest that the cohesion issue be excluded from the Inter Governmental Conference on EMU. Although the explanation for this weakening of the link between EMU and cohesion is primarily political, we saw in Section 4 some analytical arguments, concerning the effects of exchange rate changes, which has contributed to this. However, it should be noted that there remain analytical arguments which suggest that movement to EMU should be accompanied by more developed cohesion policies.

First, while macroeconomic analysis has indeed weakened faith in the exchange rate instrument, developments in the economics of integration have heightened our understanding of the degree to which economic integration constrains national economic policies across a wide spectrum. This new understanding was outlined in Section 1 (iii) — when considering the extent to which a genuine common market required positive integration, i.e., harmonised policies in place of uncoordinated national policies. This fundamentally important observation about the integration of modern mixed-economy democracies was well explained by Pelkmans and Robson in their review of the Commission's single market White Paper.

> An undiluted application of the principle of free movement for factors and products — which would involve not merely the negative abolition of restrictions but the elaboration of many 'positive' measures — would inevitably, through its impact on the 'effective jurisdiction' of Member States, drastically undermine the delicately balanced packages of public policy regulation, market intervention, income redistribution measures and macroeconomic policies that are at present determined at the level of national politics (Pelkmans and Robson, 1987).

But this suggests that the connection between monetary union and cohesion — previously based on the idea that Community budgetary mechanisms must replace national exchange rate policy — remains valid because of the close connection between economic, monetary and political integration which is revealed by the new understanding of the integration of mixed economies.

The second reason why we should not accept a severing of the connection between monetary union and the cohesion issue is that the inability of exchange rate changes to influence employment, output and unemployment should not be taken too far. While very small countries, with very open economies, may have limited ability to use the exchange rate instrument this is not equally true of all countries which will join EMU. The purpose of the Treaty revision is to devise a system of economic management which will be capable of dealing with the variety of existing circumstances and unforeseen events in the Community.

Evaluation of the Irish Government's Approach

At first sight, the Irish government's approach to the cohesion issue might seem to be open to the criticism that, although the accompanying paper referred to the ultimate need for budgetary systems "analogous to those in existing unions", the proposed Treaty revisions suggest merely a strengthening of the existing Community approach to cohesion, i.e., the Structural Funds. In the same vein, it might be argued that the Spanish government has adopted a more vigorous and analytical approach — reminding governments and the Commission that the question of EMU and the Community budget were, until very recently, seen as interlinked – and that there are good analytical arguments for this connection. In comparison with the Spanish government's approach, it might seem as if the Irish government is not quite convinced of the broader understanding of cohesion advocated by NESC and would, perhaps, prefer a further increase in the Structural Funds with some widening of eligibility. Once that preference is chosen then the Treaty revisions such as those proposed by the Irish government follow, given the fact that Structural Fund allocations are decided by secondary legislation not by Treaty provision. Those who see limits to the potential of the Structural Funds may question this approach.

Any such criticism must have regard to a number of factors. The first factor is tactical. It involves a judgement of what alliance of forces, either member states or the Commission, is available to support a development of the cohesion issue in the current context. Several national governments are certainly hostile, and in these circumstances, a medium-term view which relies on the Commission might be justified. Although the Commission has, in the run up to the IGCs, let political considerations occlude the cohesion issue, it has nevertheless put on record its awareness of the need for development of the Community budget, as we saw above. In these circumstances a tactical case could be made for the approach adopted by the Irish government.

Second, the potential for a more vigorous and radical approach by the Irish government may be constrained by the limited ambition of the 1991 IGCs. We noted several times that in many reports and analyses the move to EMU was linked to the introduction of a wider, budgetary, approach to cohesion. However, implicit in this linkage was the idea that the move to EMU would mark a substantial political development, as the Community established political bodies with the requisite legitimacy and capacity to formulate the economic policy of the union. In that context the emergence of an automatic budgetary cohesion instrument would be as much a concomitant of the deeper economic and political union as a conscious effort to reduce regional disparities. If the IGCs of 1991 had this level of ambition then it would be surprising if the Irish government, among others, did not make a vigorous attempt to advance the fiscal union. However, it now seems likely that the new Treaty will be a very modest advance on the Single Act where political and economic union are concerned, and that introduction of monetary union may not be accompanied by significant development of the Community's economic policy. Indeed, many are now of the opinion that a further Treaty revision will occur in a few years time. In this context, it might be argued that there was little to be gained from an aggressive approach to cohesion by the Irish government.

Another way of putting this point, and expressing the parallel between political union and the cohesion issue, is to note one way in which the perception of political union has itself changed. It has traditionally been thought that political union was a definable degree of political integration. The evidence of recent years and of the 1991 IGCs suggests that political union has become a process and that everything which depends on it, including cohesion, must be viewed similarly. Indeed, in this context it should be said that the new Treaty provision for tri-annual Commission reports on progress towards cohesion contains considerable potential if the political development of the Community continues to progress and if a sufficiently strong case can be made at both the analytical and political levels.

However, it is not enough to cite the limited political ambition of the political union IGC as explanation and defence of the treatment of the cohesion issue. A distinction can be made between the ambition of the IGCs and the direction in which they point the Community, and it seems important to establish that the Community is going *in the direction of existing unions,* even if the distance travelled is, for the present, to be very little. But, establishing this involves establishing that the Community will become involved in a wider range of economic policies; here one would meet resistance, not only because of reluctance to devote more resources to the Community budget (and see them used to promote cohesion), but mainly because of a refusal, on the part of various member governments, to yield (perceived) sovereignty over certain economic policies. Indeed, it is important to see that the change in the approach to cohesion in EMU parallels a change in the view on the degree to which economic policy coordination is necessary for EMU.

A further consideration which is relevant to any comparison between the Spanish and Irish approaches at the 1991 IGC is that the Spanish paper was not entirely clear analytically and the main concrete proposal may amount to little more than an argument for additional Structural Funds.

In conclusion, although at first sight the Spanish government's approach might seem more closely, or at least more wholeheartedly, based on the analytical ideas sketched above, this may not be correct. There is a sense in which the Irish government's approach can be seen to be consistent with that analysis: the very limits of the ambition of the 1991 IGCs suggests that the degree of political cohesion is not about to be greatly increased and, on the analysis of this paper, this limits the progress that can be made on economic and social cohesion. Consequently, the real issue about the Irish government's approach may lie elsewhere.

Political Homogeneity

That real issue may concern the importance of an overall approach to the two IGCs which is sufficiently oriented to creating that degree of political cohesion or political homogeneity which would be necessary for a significant development of the cohesion issue along the lines outlined above. In saying that "it is not realistic to see cohesion . . . as a purely economic phenomenon which can be achieved prior to or independently of 'political homogeneity'" NESC may have been suggesting that the positions on a wide range of issues — economic policy, political union, security, defence and institutional balance — are best decided together by reference to a guiding strategic approach to European integration.

(v) Issues for the Future

A Perspective on the Current Place of the Cohesion Issue

Section 2 contained a discussion of the place of the cohesion issue in the Community system — noting that the relationship between the regional objective and the common market objective is largely a product of the relationship between the Community and the member states. Section 3 studied the situation of the cohesion question in the 1991 IGCs and in the new Treaty; identifying a change in the place of cohesion in political discussion at Community level, in particular, a decoupling of EMU from cohesion. There the question arose of whether this implies a change in the position in the real politics of the Community. I now try to answer this question – drawing, where necessary, on the earlier arguments.

It seems highly unlikely that the cohesion issue has, in fact, been down-graded in the Community. First, the Commission's recent tendency to avoid the issue is largely a political expedient intended to minimise opposition to EMU. Indeed, regular review of cohesion and its policies is now inevitable. Second, the correct perspective is not so much that the issue has been down-graded, but that it has not been sufficiently developed at a time when it might have been. It is important to note that I do not base this idea, that the cohesion issue needs to be developed, on any claim that present developments will necessarily have dire consequences on regional disparities – although they could. Rather, the argument is that the cohesion question needs to be up-graded, or reformulated, because its existing place in the Community system will necessarily be changed by 1992 and EMU. First, the completion of the single market will change the existing approach to regional problems in Europe because a very large part of that approach consists of national, regional and sectoral policies. These cannot continue as before if non-tariff barriers are to be removed. Second, the creation of EMU will alter the existing place of cohesion in the overall system because it will certainly constrain a wide range of national policies. It follows that cohesion issues will inevitably arise as the completion of the single market and movement to EMU disrupt the current uncoordinated set of national approaches. The question is what ideas will be available in the coming years, and if there is a need for further Treaty revision.

Looking to the Future

With a view to the evolving nature of the Community, and of the cohesion issue within the Community system, NESC made two points which are very pertinent in the current situation. First, given the limits of current understanding of regional development, and the associated limits of structural policies, there is an urgent need for greater knowledge and more policy analysis. NESC argues that Ireland must make a leading contribution to the formulation of policies to address the problems of less developed regions. Some of the issues which need to be considered are mentioned below. But, to date, neither Irish policy makers nor economists can claim to be leaders in the analysis of regional problems and the formulation of cohesion policies.

Second, NESC points out that the process of determining Community priorities occurs not only in the European Council, but also in the Commission, the Parliament and, most importantly, *in the society at large.* A perfect example is the priority given to the single market in recent years. This implies that if the cohesion issue is to be established as a higher Community priority in the coming years, both the importance and, very significantly, the feasibility of effective common policies must, as NESC puts it, "be advocated by arguments of the highest quality in the widest possible forum" (NESC, 1989, p. 540).

Some Fundamental Questions about Cohesion

Here very brief mention is made of some of the questions which need to be considered in the analysis of the regional issue. The first of these arises because there are problems in the measurement of regional disparities and the specification of regional goals. In the Community the basic indicator of regional inequality is average regional income per head. It is well known that such measures of regional inequality depend on the regional boundaries which are chosen. While this is a statistical property of any set of averages, it is important to see that it also reflects a real property of the economy and society.

That real property is the relationship between regional and social inequality. The pursuit of regional equality only makes sense if the reduction of regional inequality also implies the reduction of social or inter-personal inequality. The pursuit of inter-regional equality or equity has been characterised as substituting 'place prosperity' for the more fundamental goal of 'people prosperity'.

This has a definite relevance to Ireland and to the role of Community regional and social policy. One of the major reasons why Ireland qualifies, on income and other grounds, for Structural Funds is that over 16 per cent of the workforce is unemployed. In the absence of analysis of the relationship between regional equity and social equity there is serious possibility that the goals of Community structural policy are meaningless.

If there are problems in defining regions, regional welfare and regional interests, there are equivalent problems concerning regional policy which need to be examined. The success of regional policy is dependent on a correct understanding of the causes of the cohesion problems which are defined as regional problems. Regional policy, that is policy which manipulates the location of economic activity, will only work if location or distance are important determinants of regional development. While this is virtually assumed in undertaking regional policy it needs, in fact, to be analysed.

In Ireland's case, the need is for analysis of the nature and significance of peripherality. It should not be assumed, as it is in both Ireland and the Commission, that Ireland's competitive disadvantage consists of, or is explained by, peripherality or, put another way, that the phenomenon of peripherality boils down to distance. It is arguable that these rather fundamental questions concerning regional development and regional policy need to be considered if really effective Community policies are to be devised. Pursuit of these questions implies, by definition, a rejection of any notion that progress on the cohesion issue consists in, or is measured by, Ireland's net budgetary receipts from the Community.

BIBLIOGRAPHY

Commission (1990a), *Economic and Monetary Union.* Luxembourg: Office for Publications of the European Communities.

Commission (1990b), *One market, One Money: an evaluation of the potential benefits and costs of forming an economic and monetary union. European Economy,* No. 44, October.

Corden, W. (1972), 'Monetary Integration', *Essays in International Finance,* No. 93, Princeton University.

Delors, J. (1989), *Report on Economic and Monetary Union in the European Community.* Luxembourg: Office for Official Publications of the European Communities.

Eichengreen, B. (1990), 'One Money for Europe? Lessons from the US Currency Union', *Economic Policy,* No. 10.

Goodhart, C. A. E. (1989), *Money, Information and Uncertainty.* Second edition. London: Macmillan.

Gore, C. (1984), *Regions in Question: space, development theory and regional policy.* London: Methuen.

Keeble, D., Owens, P. L. and Thompson, C. (1982), 'Regional Accessability and Economic Potential in the European Community', *Regional Studies,* Vol. 16, No. 6.

Krugman, P. (1987), 'Economic Integration in Europe: conceptual issues', T. Padoa-Schioppa (ed.), *Efficiency, Stability and Equity: a strategy for the evolution of the economic system of the European Community.* Oxford: Oxford University Press.

Krugman, P. (1989), 'Increasing Returns and Economic Geography', NBER Working Paper, No. 3275, March.

Laffan, B. (1984), 'The Politics of Redistribution in the European Community', *Administration,* Vol. 32, No. 2.

MacDougall, D. (1977), *Report of the Study Group on the Role of Public Finance in European Integration,* Vols. 1 and 2 (The MacDougall Report). Brussels: European Commission.

NESC (1989), *Ireland in the European Community: Performance, Prospects and Strategy.* Dublin: National Economic and Social Council.

O'Donnell, R. (1991), 'Monetary Policy' in *Ireland and EC Membership Evaluated,* P. Keatinge (ed.). London: Pinter.

OECD (1987), *Structural Adjustment and Economic Performance*. Paris: OECD.

Padoa-Schioppa, T. (1987), *Efficiency, Stability and Equity: a strategy for the evolution of the economic system of the European Community*. Oxford: Oxford University Press.

Pelkmans, J. and Robson, P. (1987), 'The Aspirations of the White Paper', *Journal of Common Market Studies*, Vol. 25, No. 3.

Scott, A. J. and Storper, M. (1986), *Production, Work, Territory: the geographical anatomy of industrial capitalism*. Boston: Allen and Unwin.

Vanhove, N. and Klaassen, L. H. (1987), *Regional Policy: a European Perspective*. Second edition. London: Gower.

Werner, P. (1970), *Economic and Monetary Union in the Community*. Luxembourg: Office for Official Publications of the European Communities.

LIST OF ABBREVIATIONS

CAP	Common Agricultural Policy
CB	Central Bank
DIRT	Deposit Interest Retention Tax
DM	Deutschmark
EAGGF	European Agricultural Guarantee and Guidance Fund
EC	European Community
ECB	European Central Bank
ECOFIN	Council of Economic and Finance Ministers
ECSC	European Coal and Steel Community
EEC	European Economic Community
EMF	European Monetary Fund
EMS	European Monetary System
EMU	Economic and Monetary Union
ERDF	European Regional Development Fund
ESCB	European System of Central Banks
ESF	European Social Fund
ESRI	Economic and Social Research Institute
GDP	Gross Domestic Product
IGC	Inter Governmental Conference
IMF	International Monetary Fund
NESC	National Economic and Social Council
OECD	Organisation for Economic Cooperation and Development
SF	Structural Funds

AUTHORS' BIOGRAPHIES

Tomás F. Ó Cofaigh, LL.D., is President of the Economic and Social Research Institute. He was educated at the O'Connell Schools and Trinity College, Dublin. He began his career in 1939 when he entered the Civil Service, Department of Defence; he served in the Department of Finance from 1948. He was Secretary of the latter department 1977–81; Director 1977–81 and Governor 1981–87 of the Central Bank of Ireland. Dr. Ó Cofaigh has held appointments in a number of international financial institutions: Alternate Governor for Ireland, World Bank 1977–81 and International Monetary Fund 1981–87; Member EEC Monetary Committee 1974–76; Member Committee of Governors of EC Central Banks and Board of Governors of the European Monetary Cooperation Fund 1981–87 (Chairman of both in 1984). He was also, at various times, a Member of the National Economic and Social Council and from 1987 to 1989 was Chairman of the Government Marketing Group for Dublin's International Financial Services Centre. He has been a Member of the Board of Irish Life since 1988.

Rory O'Donnell is a Senior Research Officer at the Economic and Social Research Institute, Dublin. He was previously economist at Ireland's National Economic and Social Council, where he prepared the Council's report *Ireland in the European Community: Performance, Prospects and Strategy* (1989). His publications include *Adam Smith's Theory of Value and Distribution* (1990) and articles on the economics of European integration. He received his Ph.D. in economics from the University of Cambridge and has taught there and at University College, Dublin and University College, Galway.

Patrick Honohan is a Research Professor at the Economic and Social Research Institute in Dublin since November 1990. Dr. Honohan spent the previous three years at the World Bank working on financial sector issues. Previously he had spent more than ten years in the Irish public service, at the Central Bank of Ireland and as Economic Advisor to the Taoiseach. He received his Ph.D. in Economics from the London School of Economics and has taught economics there and at the University of California, San Diego, the Australian National University, and University College, Dublin.